SURAH AL-FATHIHA
(THE OPENING, QURAN)

In the name of God, the Beneficent, the Merciful. Praise be to God, Lord of the worlds, the Beneficent, the Merciful: Owner of the day of judgment, You (alone) do we worship; You alone do we ask for help. Show us the straight path, the path of those whom You have favored; not (the path) of those who earn Your anger nor of those who go astray.

Easily
Understand Islam
— Finally I get it!
— A collection of articles—

Compiled by F. Kamal

The following statements are noted in conformance with the request of the copyright holder:
New Revised Standard Version Bible, copyright 1989, Division of Christian Education of the National Council of the Churches of Christ in the United States of America. Used by permission. All rights reserved.

Sahih Muslim and Sunan Abu Dawud English translation quotes used with permission of Sh. Muhammad Ashraf Publisher.

Mention of associations, websites, authorities and individuals in this book does not necessarily imply endorsement, nor does it imply that the associations, websites, authorities and individuals endorse each other or this book.

This book is intended to provide accurate information with regard to the subject matter covered. However, any work may contain errors. No responsibility is accepted by the publisher or author(s) for inaccuracies, omissions, or typographical or other errors. Nor is it implied that reading this book will result any earnings (or any other) benefits for the reader. The author(s) and publisher specifically disclaim any loss, risk, or liability, whether personal, legal, financial, or otherwise, direct or indirect, incurred under any theory of liability, as a consequence, from the use and/or application of any of this book's contents. Testimonials reflect views and submissions at the time we receive them. Individual testimonials do not necessarily imply endorsement by the institutions or entities associated with the individuals.

ISBN-13: 978-1-59236-011-6
ISBN-10: 1-59236-011-4

Publisher's Cataloging-in-Publication
(Provided by Quality Books, Inc.)

>   Easily understand Islam : finally I get it! : a collection
>   of articles / compiled by F. Kamal. -- 1st ed.
>   p. cm.
>   Includes bibliographical references and index.
>   LCCN 2005931368
>   ISBN 1-59236-011-4
>
>   1. Islam.   I. Kamal, F., 1963-
>
>   BP161.3.E27 2005   297
>   QBI05-600143

Publisher: Desert Well Network LLC
http://www.DesertWellNetwork.com
Printed in USA.

Table of Contents

SECTION IV: OTHER TOPICS

SECTION V: ISLAMIC RESOURCES

Note to Readers

The chapters are fairly independent of each other. Those pressed for time, or seeking a quick snapshot, may jump directly to the topics most interesting to them, after reading the first two chapters. The wide scope presented by the chapters is for the convenience of the reader, allowing one to easily find many disparate topics under "one roof". While one should not feel obligated to finish the book in one reading, reading the book in sequence, in its entirety, is likely to be the smoothest and most fulfilling experience, with the least likelihood of misunderstandings.

Since this a collection of articles, different authors may have followed different styles and conventions. For example, Koran, Quran, Qu'ran, Qu'raan are all valid but different spellings of the Muslim Holy book. Typically in Muslim writings, abbreviations of respect such pbuh (peace be upon him) , raa, swt (subhanah wa ta'ala, glory be to Him in the Highest) follow the names of prophets, companions of the prophet, and God respectively. Since this interrupts the flow for first time non-Muslim readers they are omitted, but should be assumed to be present implicitly. Religious references typically refer to the Quran or collections of the sayings of prophet Muhammad. The pronoun "he" or "him" has been used occasionally in a gender neutral manner to avoid awkward he/she syntax.

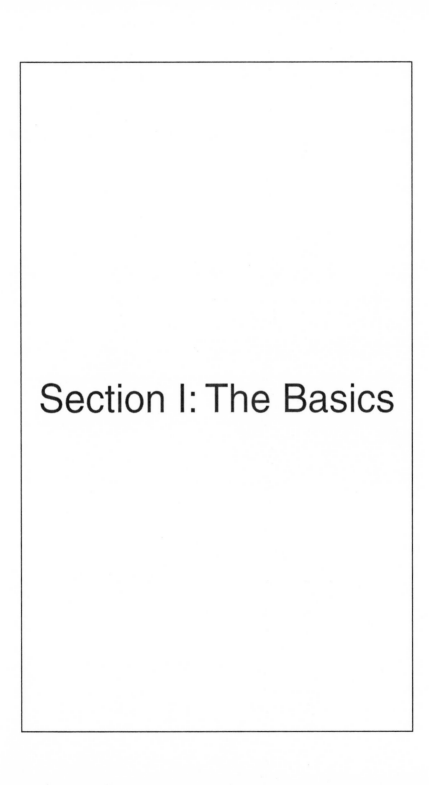

Section I: The Basics

In the Name of God, Most Gracious, Most Merciful,

By (the Token of) time (through the Ages)

Verily Man is in loss

Except such as have Faith and do righteous deeds and (join together) in the mutual teaching of Truth and of Patience and Constancy.

Quran, Surah Al-Asr

What Islam is Not

Top Misconceptions about Islam

By F. Kamal

MISCONCEPTION #1

NOTION

Muslims worship some weird god.

MUSLIM POSITION

Muslims worship the same God that prophet Abraham and prophet Moses worshipped . There is no difference. Just as "Dieu" is the French word for God, "Allah", the term preferred for use by Muslims for God, is basically the word "God" in Arabic. (It translates literally as "The God," reflecting a very heavy emphasis on monotheism.) Muslims prefer to use the term Allah for a variety of reasons. For example, the word God can be the root for god, god(s), god(dess), god(father), god(mother). But the word Allah does not lend itself to such forms. Note: In Aramaic, the language Jesus spoke, the word for

God is "Aalah" whose pronunciation is very similar to the Arabic "Allah." [1] Aramaic is a sister language to Arabic.

Muslims believe there is only one God. The Creator of the universe. The Supreme Being. The only Absolute. The Merciful and the Beneficent. The All Knowing. The Just. The Loving. The Incomparable. The Source of Goodness. The Source of all Power. The Everlasting. In short, God is God.

MISCONCEPTION #2

NOTION
Muslims do not believe in Heaven and Hell.

MUSLIM POSITION
In fact, not only do Muslims believe in Heaven and Hell and the Day of Judgment, they also believe in the angels and that Abraham, Noah, Moses, Solomon, David, Jacob, Joseph, Jesus, and Muhammad were all prophets of God.

MISCONCEPTION #3

NOTION
Prophet Muhammad is to Islam what Jesus Christ is to Christianity – hence sometimes the (incorrect) term "Muhammadan" used to describe followers of Islam.

MUSLIM POSITION
Muslims do not worship Muhammad. They believe he is merely a servant of God, a great prophet and the final messenger of God to man. Islam is strictly

monotheistic and worships God alone. Islam means to submit to the will of God. A Muslim is one who submits to the will of God. One of the Arabic roots of the word Islam is salam (peace), and Muslims find peace in following and worshiping God.

MISCONCEPTION #4

NOTION
Islam somehow seems to promote "terrorism".

MUSLIM POSITION
Muslims would argue that this is fundamentally untrue. Muslims would say that Islam is rooted in justice and compassion and that it categorically does NOT support the deliberate torture and/ or oppression, and/or captivity and/or killing of innocent individuals. In fact, regardless of whether these actions are committed by governments, nations, groups, and/or individuals, such actions would simply be viewed as wrong –whoever did them. Also, Muslims argue, terrorists by definition, treat life as cheap but that in Islam, life is a sacred trust. Muslims would point out that life is so cherished in Islam that the Quran records, "whoever saves the life of one person, it shall be as if he had saved the life of all mankind."

MISCONCEPTION #5

NOTION
Confusing Islam with a particular culture or the actions of particular individuals.

MUSLIM POSITION

Arguably this is the most frequent mistake and certainly a very common one. Like people of other religions, Muslims are of various stripes, some devout, some casual, and yet others whose actions are frequently unislamic. Muslims would remind people that just because one meets someone calling himself a Muslim who behaves in a certain way, it does not mean that his actions reflect Islam. One way to understand this is to consider the various cases of Christian priests sexually molesting little boys. Do such actions reflect Christianity? What about white supremacists who distort Christianity to further their cause and terrorize people, does that mean their actions are Christian? Most people would rightly say: "Of course not!" Muslims would simply ask that they be judged by a similar standard. "Unislamic actions committed by Muslims do not define Islam" would be their response. In other words, "Muslim" does not always equal "Islam." In fact, since Islam is not based on mere opinion, it is quite easy to identify Islamic positions on various topics. Islam is primarily based on the Quran (the word of God, as revealed to Prophet Muhammad through Archangel Gabriel) and Sunnah (the example of the Prophet, his authentic recorded sayings (hadith) and life (seerah)). The ulema (Islamic scholars) study these sources and use a specific methodology to detail Islamic positions on various issues.

Muslims have even been admonished in Quran 60:5 "Our Lord! Make *us* [Muslims] not a [test and] trial for non-Muslims" indicating that the unislamic actions of some Muslims can sometimes confuse others who are not knowledgeable about Islam, This is a source of genuine concern to practicing Muslims. Muslims would suggest that if you want to learn about Islam, look to the Quran and Sunnah (example of the prophet) and practicing, devout Muslims.

Compiler's Note: It might even be a good idea to keep the last misconception in mind while reading this book. For example, the chapter "Islam and Racism" does not suggest that no symptoms of racism can be found within any group of over a billion Muslims. Rather in should be noted that Muslims who engage in such unislamic acts do not behave islamically. Remember, this book is entitled "Easily Understand Islam" not "Easily Understand Muslims".

Endnotes
[1] See www.Easily-Understand-islam.com/soundsame.htm

Chapter 1

2

What Is Islam?

By F. Kamal

Islam is a way of life. It is simple, practical, and easy to understand.

FIVE PILLARS
Islam is based on five pillars.

ONE

To declare "There is no deity but God, and Muhammad is the messenger of God." Islam is based primarily on the holy book for Muslims: the Quran (the word of God), and secondarily on the authentic sunnah (the example of the prophet).

Note: The *ulema* (Islamic scholars) have historically played an important role as leaders in Muslim societies and in explaining (called *tafsir*) the Quran and the *sunnah* (life and example) of the Prophet. *Of themselves*, however, they do not have the authority to forgive or to define right (halal) or wrong (haram). Rather they help elucidate concepts and define principles. There is no priesthood in Islam. A Muslim does not have to have any "intermediary" between himself and God.

TWO

Salat: To worship God in prayer five times a day.

THREE

Sawm: To fast during the month of Ramadan. (The purpose of fasting in Islam during Ramadan is not penance for sins, but rather to develop *taqwa* —God-consciousness.)

FOUR

Zakat: To give charity to the poor.

FIVE

Hajj: To perform pilgrimage to Mecca once in a lifetime *if* one has the financial means and health to do so.

Note: It is important to recognize that God does not "need" or "require" anything from His creation. God is not a "needy god." That would be to misunderstand God's Power and Majesty. Thus, worship, for example, is for the benefit of the worshiper not God. And indeed prayer disciplines, purifies, and elevates the worshipper.

ISLAMIC ARTICLES OF FAITH
There are six basic articles of faith.

ONE

To believe in God.

TWO

His Angels.

THREE

His Apostles (like Abraham, Noah, Jacob, Joseph, Job, Jonah, David, Solomon, Moses, and Jesus) .

FOUR

His revealed books (e.g. Taurat, Zabur to David, Injeel to Jesus, & Quran). (According to Muslim belief, only the Quran –alternative spellings: Qur'an or Koran – however is available today in an original, pure form.)

FIVE

To believe in resurrection, the Day of Judgment, and Heaven and Hell.

SIX

Divine Decree: That God is omniscient (All Knowing) and has power over all things.

EXCELLENCE (IHSAN)

Another important aspect of Islam is "ihsan" (meaning excellence or to seek to do things in a best and beautiful manner).

A Muslim is called to live his life in the most excellent and beautiful of manners because even if he does not physically see God, God always sees him. Whether one is an engineer, doctor, homemaker, bricklayer, or street sweeper, one should always try to discharge oneself with excellence.

For example, does not someone who is brought before the head of his company endeavor to comport himself in a way to put himself forward in the best possible light? How much more should one do, if it is not a mere mortal boss, but the One who sits on the throne of the universe, that one stands before?

A Muslim's journey through life should strive to continuously pulsate with excellence and beauty. After all, this is a part of being Muslim. [1}

WHO IS A MUSLIM?

If you believe, sincerely in your heart, the five pillars and the articles of faith you are a Muslim. It is that simple!

SUMMARY

For Muslims, Islam is a very simple, practical, and balanced religion. One can communicate directly with God. There is no need for intermediaries like priests. There is no sharp delineation between worldly and spiritual realms. Perhaps an illustrative example of this is that, while some religious traditions may have encouraged clerical celibacy amongst their religious hierarchy Islam in contrast encourages marriage amongst its adherents. "Marriage is one half your deen [e.g. religion]" (Baihaqi) is well known among Muslims. Almost all Muslim leaders have been married (and usually with lots of children!). Muslims thus view their religion as practical -- and as a mercy from God.

Religion is not seen as something special to be isolated from life but as an integral part of everyday life. Islam is not an abstract idealism but rather a complete way of life well within the grasp and understanding of the average individual. It forms the dynamic core of societal life in active Muslim communities.

Muslims would say that following Islam is like returning to a natural and intuitive path for humans that leads to peace and contentment of the soul.

Endnotes
[1] An-Nawawi's Forty Hadith, Hadith #2, mentions the pillars, articles of faith and ihsan in describing Islam. (It also mentions being aware of man's signposts in the journey towards the culmination of human existence.) .

Chapter 2

Section II: General Articles

Mishkat ul Masabih #261: 'Aun reported that 'Abdullah b. Mas'ud said: There are two avaricious persons who are never contented. The man of learning and the man of the world, but the two are not equal; the man of knowledge increases in submission to God, but the man of the world becomes head strong and defiant. 'Abdullah then recited: "Nay, man is surely rebellious when he sees himself free from want" (Quran 46:6); concerning the other he cited the verse: Surely those of His servants who are possessed of knowledge, fear God (Quran 35:28) (Darimi).

Islam & Racism

By F. Kamal

When people have exploited, oppressed, and subjugated each other solely based on gender, class, nationality, or race it has led to much suffering on our planet throughout long periods of our history. Such artificial distinctions reflect false pride or arrogance. False pride or arrogance is a trait repugnant to devout Muslims.

It is instructive to note that the *first* introduction of the evil Iblis (Satan) in the Quran finds him rebelling against His Lord in arrogance. *Quran 2:34* states: "And behold, We said to the angels, 'Bow down to Adam,' and they bowed down. Not so Iblis, he refused and was haughty. He was of those who reject Faith." The Quran elaborates in *Quran 7:12.* (God) said, "What prevented you from prostrating when I commanded you?" He said, "I am better than he. You created me from fire, and him from clay." (Are these words too different from today's racist if you substitute fire and clay with the appropriate words?)

The Quran continues in the next ayah, *Quran 7:13*. (God) said, "Get down from here, it is not for you to be arrogant here, get out, for you are of the meanest (of creatures)." As Muslims would note, how can any devout Muslim accept expressions of false pride or arrogance when the Quran says in *Quran 17:53*: "Say to My servants that they should (only) say those things that are best for Satan sows dissensions among them, because Satan is to man an avowed enemy."[1}

Islam categorically and unequivocally dismisses *all* these artificial distinctions of rank. In fact, one of the core pillars of Islam – the Hajj — illustrates this vividly.

Once in a lifetime, if one is financially and physically able, a Muslim must perform the Hajj. During this spiritual journey, Muslims leave behind their worldly effects and put on a very simple garb. During Hajj it is not possible to tell the difference between a millionaire and a pauper, a ruler and a subject. Hundreds of thousands of people from all races, backgrounds and all corners of the globe come together simply for one purpose: to glorify and obey their Creator and Lord. This reminds people of their true relationship with God.

Islam is one of the very few movements that has had a great deal of success in helping to eradicate the scourge of racism from the hearts of men. Noteworthy is the story of Malcolm X, a famous American civil rights leader. An African American revert (convert) to Islam, Malcolm X had originally believed that whites were devils. He had been filled with anger at the terrible injustice suffered by blacks at the hands of whites in America. Yet when he encountered Islam it transformed his life. This is what he said about Islam and about a Hajj he made.

"Never have I witnessed such sincere hospitality and such overwhelming spirit of true brotherhood as is practiced by people of all colors and races here in this Ancient Holy Land, the home of Abraham and all the other Prophets of Holy scriptures. For the past week I have been truly speechless and spellbound by the graciousness I see displayed all around me by people of all colors. I have been blessed to visit the Holy City of Mecca. ... There were tens of thousands of pilgrims, from all over the world. They were of all colors, from blue eyed blonds to black skinned Africans. But we were all practicing in the same ritual, displaying a spirit of unity and brotherhood that my experiences in America had led me to believe never could exist between the white and the non-white.

America needs to understand Islam, because this is the one religion that erases from its society the race problem. Throughout my travels in the Muslim world, I have met, talked to, even eaten with people who in America would have been considered 'white', but the 'white' attitude had been removed from their minds by the religion of Islam. I have never before seen such sincere and true brotherhood, practiced by all colors together, irrespective of their color.

You may be shocked by these words coming from me. But on this pilgrimage, what I have seen and experienced has forced me to re-arrange much of the thought patterns previously held, and to toss aside some of my previous conclusions. ... Despite my firm convictions, I have always been a man who tries to face facts, and to accept the reality of life as new experience and new knowledge unfolds. I have always kept an open mind, which is necessary to the flexibility that must go hand in hand with every form of the intelligent search for truth. ...

I could see from this, that perhaps if white Americans could accept the oneness of God, then perhaps, too, they could accept in reality the Oneness of Man—and cease to measure, and hinder, and harm others in terms of their 'differences' in color." [2]

When reading Malcolm's words, and knowing about the tremendous personal transformation he went through, one is reminded of the following two Quranic ayat (verses), which are well worth reading. They will be of interest for all those who have been hurt by the cruelty of racism. Others have found them to be a source of healing for anger, resentment and pain.

We send down (stage by stage) in the Qur'an a *healing* and a mercy to those who believe (Quran 17:82)

Verily in the remembrance of God do hearts find rest! (Quran 13:28).

An interesting surah (Quranic chapter) is Surah Yusuf (Joseph) in the Quran. It discusses sabr (patient perseverance) and placing one's trust in God. Here we read about the vastly different scales humans and God may use to value an individual's life. In Quran 12;20, we read about prophet Yusuf being sold. "The (brothers) sold him for a miserable price, for a few coins counted out. In such low estimation did they hold him!" Yet God held him in such estimation that he made Yusuf a prophet! A surah with great wisdom.

The Quran clearly dismisses all metrics of rank between men, except one, and that metric is righteousness, God-consciousness. The following Quranic ayah clearly establishes this Islamic concept definitively and emphatically.

O mankind! We created you from a single (pair) of a male and a female, and made you into nations and tribes, so that you may know each other [3] [(not that you may despise (each other).] Verily the most honored of you in the sight of God is (he who is) the most righteous of you. And God has full knowledge and is well acquainted (with all things). (Quran 49:13)

Said Prophet Muhammad in the last sermon:

All mankind is from Adam and Eve, an Arab has no superiority over a non-Arab, nor does a non-Arab have any superiority over an Arab; also a white has no superiority over a black, nor a black has any superiority over a white except by piety and good action.

Chapter end notes.

[1] Note: In Islam, "Satan" is generally not believed to be an angel. Rather he is a "jinn" who was amongst the group of angels being addressed. (Also see Quran 18:50 which is a more detailed account.) Jinn, can have different meanings, but normally refers to a different creation from either humans or angels.
[2] From THE AUTOBIOGRAPHY OF MALCOLM X by Malcolm X and Alex Haley, copyright © 1964 by Alex Haley and Malcolm X. Copyright (c) 1965 by Alex Haley and Betty Shabazz. Used by permission of Random House, Inc.

[3] The phrase "so that you may know one another" has also been interpreted as "that you may exchange knowledge" or "that you may exchange favors." As a fun, offbeat aside there is an interesting theory in modern economics that was put forward by classical economist David Ricardo. It states that two nations should trade with each other even if one country does *everything* better than the other country. Even though the first country does everything better than the second country it can get more "bang for the buck" by diverting some of its resources into its higher margin products than its lower margin products. By trading with the second nation, some of the first nation's resources (most importantly: time) are freed up allowing for the diversion. Thus both nations benefit by the trade. (Of course, contemporary economists have suggested minor "tweaks" to the central idea of free trade. So, for example, in some scenarios it may be permissible to offer some protection to emerging, nascent native industries. Global trade can increase the "pie" (e.g. overall net wealth) but there need to be mechanisms to ensure proper circulation of the wealth gains. Allocating some gains towards education (e.g. future productivity), cushioning short term allocation shocks, and preventing excessive wealth concentrating into non-productive population segments and monitoring and/or compensating for any explicit or implicit subsidies, may also be other ideas worth exploring along with globalization.)

Why is there Evil and Suffering?

By F. Kamal

Note: If non-Muslims are reading this chapter please be aware, that this article was *originally written for a Muslim audience* and that unfortunately, it may sometimes be difficult to fully understand some matters "vicariously." Even many Muslims find that Islam is often best understood when actually practiced (with sincerity). It is however offered as an insight for interested individuals. (So do consult with knowledgeable Muslims if you do not understand something here.)

Why is there evil in this world? Why is there suffering? Isn't everything just plain unfair? Why are a Muslim's duas [supplications] not answered?

Answer # 1

What causes evil? What causes darkness but the absence of light? Where can light come from if not from one's Lord and Creator? Who is the wanton murderer and torturer but someone who has chosen to turn away from his Lord and thus condemns himself to be left stumbling in his own darkness? Where is there light except where God spreads it with His Grace on those who have submitted completely to their Lord -- in full love and awe of Him?

Thus "evil" can arise because of the freedom of choice (e.g., to submit to God or to turn away from Him in rebellion), choice given to man for a short time by God. It is this freedom that will uncloak the good from the bad. We must remember that for many the world is full of (spiritual) tests — those who do well will go to heaven, and those who fail the tests will go to hell. However, if there were no hardship or effort involved in the tests — what sort of testing would it be? How effective would it really be in separating the good from the bad? Does not "to be tested" mean to summon up all your reserves to accomplish a task?

Does an athlete become one without years of dedication, enterprise, and hard work? Should we expect endless, vast fields of happiness and wealth in paradise with no sweat, no toil, no suffering?

Where is the logic in this? If everything is okay how will anyone be tested? Everyone will seem okay. A man shows his true colors under duress and hardship. Is there any better way to mark a person for evil then to have one express one's evil? For example, if Hitler were given all the land, wealth, and fame he sought *instantly* without a trial, would we humans have known his true nature? Or would you prefer that these individuals' inner evil remain hidden to the world and themselves? How pleasant would heaven be with backbiters, murderers, thieves, and hypocrites as your bosom companions and neighbors. Can these rebellious people inhabit heaven you ask? Nay, this is not a heaven but rather a hell. How effective is the test?

Sunan Abu-Dawud Book 40, Number 4726: Narrated Abu Hurayrah: "The Apostle of God (peace be upon him) said: When God created paradise, He said to Gabriel, 'Go and look at it.' He went and looked at it, then came and said, 'O my Lord! By Your might, no one who hears of it will fail to enter it.' He then surrounded it with disagreeable things, and said, 'Go and look at it, Gabriel.' He went and looked at it, then came and said, 'O my Lord! By Your might, I am afraid that no one will enter it.' When God created hell, He said, 'Go and look at it, Gabriel.' He went and looked at it, then came and said, 'O my Lord! By Your might, no one who hears of it will enter it.' He then surrounded it with desirable things and said, 'Go and look at it, Gabriel.' He went, looked at it, then came and said, 'O my Lord! By Your might and power, I am afraid that no one will remain who does not enter it.'"

Imagine for a moment the *reverse*—the enticing things were outside heaven and the difficult things outside hell. Would the right people be in hell? How many tyrannical rulers have committed grotesque torture of their subjects, ridiculed the truth, oppressed the weak and helpless, and seized wealth beyond their needs to live in mansions, with fast cars and even faster women? The allure of the world is becoming indeed. The unscrupulous will not allow morality to stand in their way of devouring wealth and fame, surrounded by "beautiful art treasures," trying to satiate all their appetites and vices, living "the good life," "the life of ease and luxury." Would you want these people in heaven?

Consider next the "loser" who offered food to a

hungry person even though he himself had little and was hungry, or the individual who was "foolhardy" enough to fight for justice even though he could have "compromised" and found a position of power, wealth and influence oppressing those weaker than he. Consider the individual who was tortured, starved and beaten just because he tried to create a better world. Would you want these people in hell?

How do we find out the mettle of a person, what a person believes in, what he is made of? The hadith from Sunah Abu Dawud above tells you how God has chosen to mark the good from the bad, and God is Al-Alim (The Omniscient), Al-'Adl (The Just).

Quran 3:142: Did you think that you would enter Heaven without God testing those of you who fought hard (in His cause) and remained steadfast?

Quran 47:31: And We shall try you until We test those among you who strive their utmost and persevere in patience; and We shall try your reported (mettle).

Quran 2.155 -157: And surely We shall try you with something of fear and hunger, and loss of wealth and lives and crops; but give glad tidings to the steadfast, Who say, when a misfortune strikes them: "Lo! we are God's and lo! unto Him we are returning." Such are they on whom are blessings from their Lord and mercy. Such are the rightly guided.

Quran 16:96: What is with you must vanish; what is with God will endure. And We will certainly bestow, on those who patiently persevere, their reward according to the best of their actions.

Quran 29:2: Do men think that they will be left alone on saying, "We believe," and that they will not be tested?

We may be being tested even when we do not expect it, in forms we may or may not expect, as mentioned in this beautiful saying of the prophet.

Abu Huraira reported God's Messenger (may peace be upon him) as saying: Verily, God, the Exalted and Glorious, would say on the Day of Resurrection," O son of Adam, I was sick but you did not visit Me." He would say, "O my Lord; how could I visit You whereas You are the Lord of the Worlds?" Thereupon He would say, "Didn't you know that such and such servant of Mine was sick but you did not visit him and were you not aware of this that if you had visited him, you would have found Me by him? O son of Adam, I asked food from you but you did not feed Me." He would say, "My Lord, how could I feed You whereas You are the Lord of the worlds?" He said, "Didn't you know that such and such servant of Mine asked food from you but you did not feed him, and were you not aware that if you had fed him you would have found him by My side?" (The Lord would again say,) "O son of Adam, I asked drink from you but you did not provide Me." He would say, "My Lord, how could I provide You whereas You are the Lord of the Worlds?" Thereupon He would say, "Such and such of servant of Mine asked you for a drink but you did not provide him, and had you provided him drink you would have found him near Me." (Muslim 32.6232).

If one suffers, remember that the night is followed by day. "Know that with patience there is victory, with affliction there is relief, and with hardship there is ease" (Nawawi #19). See also Quran 94:5-6.

Please note that it is *impossible* for there to be full human justice on this earth. Consider the mother whose daughter has been unjustly tortured and killed. Even if (and it is a very big if) her killer is caught and imprisoned, has justice really been done? If you ask the family, they will undoubtedly note that their daughter is not back with them. Or consider a tyrannical ruler who tortured and murdered thousands of people. Even if he is caught and executed, has justice been done? Does one death equal thousands of deaths? We must remember our test on earth will for the most part establish accountability for the Day of Judgement when true justice will occur. God can do things humans cannot, and, if He wishes, He can compensate the victim and her family as He sees fit. He can also cause the tyrannical ruler to suffer the punishment of 1000 deaths, for on that day, our good and bad deeds will stand before us, awaiting judgement.

This test is for our sake, since God is Al-Alim (The Omniscient) and as such already knows the outcome (although we do have full moral freedom of choice in our actions). (see Sahih Bukhari 4.55.550). The test is for our sake. (We can image the Serb commander of a Bosnian concentration torture camp saying, "Oh I am one of the good ones! I deserve Paradise!" If there had been no worldly life, what proof would he have seen against his own statements? Yet now because of life, his deeds will stretch out before him and stand witness against him on the Day of Judgement. But God is, of course, Al-Alim (The Omniscient). One can use the analogy of the good teacher who can predict which students will pass or fail a test that he or she gives. It should be noted that even though the students have full freedom to select their answers to the test questions, that does not change the ability of a good teacher to predict passes and fails. Of course, God, who transcends time, knows and does not predict.

Answer #2

Sometimes we desire something that is, in truth, bad for us, or we despair when "hard times" strike us when in reality with just our limited knowledge, we cannot truly know if something we encounter will eventually benefit us or harm us – whether it is good for us or not—unless God tells us. Sometimes we are happy for a bad thing and complain when we really should be grateful. Perhaps sometimes God gives us what we truly need instead of what we think we want.

> *Quran 2:216:* ... but it may happen that you hate a thing that is good for you, and it may happen that you love a thing that is bad for you. God knows, you do not know.

So sometimes it is, in fact, better that we do not get what we want.

There is the story of the man who asked Prophet Muhammad to pray for him to become wealthy. The Prophet ignored him. Again he asked, and again the Prophet ignored him. Once again he asked, and so the prophet prayed that he be made wealthy. Now this individual had used to spend time at the mosque, but as his wealth grew he found himself in possession of larger and larger sheep herds. So he would take them out of the city to graze and he spent less and less time with the prophet and his companions – being preoccupied with his sheep herds. When the directive on zakat (alms giving) was revealed, the prophet sent someone to collect the zakat (charity) from him, but the man had grown so distant from Islam that he refused. Thereupon, the Prophet refused to accept any future zakat from him. Even at the time of Abu Bakr and Umar, when this man tried to pay the zakat both Caliphs (Muslim leaders) refused to accept it on the grounds that the prophet had refused zakat from him. The Prophet had sensed that wealth would not agree with this man when he had initially asked the Prophet to pray for him. Yet the man had repeatedly insisted .... Sometimes be glad you do not receive everything you ask for. Some things you ask for can lead you astray. You may not know, but God does.

In the story of Prophet Moses and Al-Khadir in the Quran (which is also explained in the hadith), God warns us about arriving at judgements based on *limited knowledge* and reminds us that absolute knowledge rest only with Him.

Sahih Bukhari volume 6, book 60, number 250: "Then a man came to Moses and asked, 'O God's Apostle! Is there anyone on the earth who is more learned than you?' Moses replied, 'No.' So God admonished him (Moses), for he did not ascribe all knowledge to God. It was said (on behalf of God), 'Yes, (there is a servant of

ours who knows more than you).'
...Then they returned back and found Al-Khadir. ...
When Moses greeted him, he uncovered his face and
said ... Who are you?' Moses said, 'I am Moses.' ... Al-
Khadir said, "What do you want?' Moses said, ' I came
to you so that you may teach me of the truth which
you were taught.' ... At that time a bird took with its
beak (some water) from the sea. Al-Khadir then said,
'By God, my knowledge and your knowledge besides
God's Knowledge is like what this bird has taken with
its beak from the sea.' "

The Quran proceeds to say what happened:

Quran 18:65–82: Then they found one of Our servants,
to whom We had given mercy from Us and had taught
him knowledge from Our presence. Moses said to him,
"May I follow you, so that you may teach me right
conduct of that which you have been taught?"He said,
"Lo! you can not bear with me. How can you bear with
what you can not compass in knowledge?" He said,
"God willing, you shall find me patient and I shall not
contradict you in any way." He said, "Well, if you go
with me, do not ask me anything until I myself bring
up the subject with you"
So the two set out. When they were in the ship, he made
a hole in it. [Moses] said, "Have you made a hole in it to
drown the passengers? Verily you have done a dreadful
thing." He said, "Did I not tell you that you could not
bear with me?" [Moses] said: "Do not be angry with
me because I forgot, and do not be hard on me for my
fault." So the two journeyed on until, when they met a
lad, he slew him. [Moses] said, "What! Have you slain
an innocent soul who has killed no man? Verily you
have done a horrid thing." He said, "Did I not tell you

that you could not bear with me?" [Moses] said: "If I ask you after this concerning anything, leave me. You have received an excuse from me."

So the two journeyed on until, when they came to the people of a certain township, they asked the people for food, but the people refused to invite them as guests. And they found in this town a wall upon the point of falling into ruin, and he repaired it. [Moses] said, "If you had wished, you could have taken payment for it."

He said, "This is the parting between you and me! I will reveal to you the interpretation of what you could not bear with patience. As for the ship, it belonged to poor people working on the river, and I wished to disable it, for there was a king behind them who is taking every ship by force. And as for the lad, his parents were believers and we feared lest he should oppress them by rebellion and disbelief. And we intended that their Lord should exchange him for one better in purity and nearer to mercy. And as for the wall, it belonged to two orphan boys in the city, and there was beneath it a treasure belonging to them, and their father had been righteous, and your Lord intended that they should come to their full strength and should bring forth their treasure as a mercy from their Lord; and I did not do it upon my own command. Such is the interpretation of what you could not bear. *(Also see Sahih Muslim, book 030, number 5865)*

We should not be envious of the life of pomp and ease enjoyed by a corrupt man of power, or discouraged by the straightened circumstances of an honest man. To call life unfair is truly foolish. To do so is to arrive at a rash judgement. Would you call the outcome of a 24 hour marathon race, 3 seconds after it had started? How accurate would your call be? Yet the life of this world is like a drop in the ocean compared to the hereafter. Says the Quran about the shortness of life of the world "(it will seem) as though they had tarried but an hour of the day" (Quran 10:45).

A human's ability to discern what is good or bad for himself is very limited. Also remember that God is al-Hakim (The Wise) and al-Latif (the Subtle One). Perhaps you asked for wisdom, and God sent you problems so you would learn wisdom, perhaps you asked for wealth and God sent you lean times to teach you the thrift you would need to build a lasting prosperity; perhaps you asked for health and God sent you health problems to teach you the value of exercise and diet to build a better foundation for your eventual good health. Remember to "trust in God. Lo! He is the Hearer, the Knower" (Quran 8:61).

Do not despair of God fulfilling your supplication, for anger and impatience about an apparent lack of results could void a supplication (Bukhari 8.354). Sometimes God surprises His pious servant with the way He chooses to help His servant.

> *Quran 65:2-3*: ... And for those who fear God, He (ever) prepares a way out, and He provides for them from (sources) they never could imagine. And if any one puts his trust in God, sufficient is (God) for him, for God will surely accomplish His purpose. Verily, for all things has God appointed a due proportion.

Sometimes God withholds the reward for your deeds. Do not despair if you do not get something you want in this life. Perhaps God will reward you with it or something better in the afterlife. The value of the afterlife after all is much, much greater then this very short life we live. Put your trust in God—for no one rewards better than He. "And [always] does He give you something out of what you may be asking of Him; and should you try to add up God's blessings, you could never count them." (Quran 14:34)

> Riyadh-us-Saleheen, #1501: Hazrat Ubadah bin Samit reports that the Holy Prophet said: "Whenever a Muslim supplicates God, He grants him his supplication, or averts some equivalent evil from him, as long as he does not pray for something sinful or something that may break the ties of kinship. Upon hearing this one of the companions said: 'Then we shall supplicate generously.' The messenger of God said: 'God is more generous in fulfilling your requests' (Tirmizi). Hakim narrating from Hazrat Abu Sa'eed, adds: 'or keeps a reward equal to his prayer in reserve for him for the Last Day.'"

How generous is our Lord who gives the believer one of three good options: 1) the boon now, 2) a similar reward in the hereafter or 3) averts an evil from us. So why should a Muslim be too concerned if he does not get option 1? This helps a Muslim understand the following saying in Abu Dawud, book 8, number 1483: Narrated Salman al-Farsi: "The Prophet (peace be upon him) said: 'Your Lord is munificent and generous, and does not want to turn away empty the hands of His servant when he raises them to Him." Truly, a pious devout servant of God can never thank

God enough for the blessings that He showers on him.

Sometimes God delays a matter in this life. God speaks about purifying from falsehood in Quran 13:17 "from that (ore) which they smelt in the fire in order to make ornaments and tools rises a foam like unto it - thus God coins (the analogy of) the true and the false." The early Muslims suffered greatly in Mecca from persecutions, mockery, torture, and banishments. When they asked the Prophet to pray for respite, he urged sabr (steadfast perseverance and patience). In the heat of these trials the good was separated from the dross. The "fire" of the trials expelled the impurities of individual Muslims like the fire expels the impurities from gold or from iron ore to create steel. The Arabic word for trial is "fitnah," which also means to test the purity of gold.

Only many years later in Medina were they strong enough to carry the awesome task of building a Muslim nation, free from the problems and limitations they had faced in Mecca. Had they been given a political community to govern earlier in their weakness, the "building" of Islam's structure would have been severely compromised. After all, steel, which is smelted from iron in heat to drive out impurities, is much stronger than iron. Perhaps this is the reason behind the hadith: Abu Hurairah reported that the Messenger of God said: "He whom God intends good, He makes him to suffer from some affliction" (Al-Bukhari). (Riyadh-us-Saleheen #39)

Sometimes God uses hardship to teach people. Take the case of a smoldering building in ruins and bullet holes, or a bankruptcy. Sometimes one's life seems to collapse completely. Says God in Quran 29:41 "The likeness of those who choose other patrons than God is as the likeness of the spider when she takes unto herself a house, and lo! the frailest of all houses is the spider's house, if they but knew." Did you build your life on a spider's web or a solid foundation built on God consciousness? Do you know what is really important in life? A solid foundation that will not crumble on you? What is ephemeral and what lasts? There is nothing stronger in life than to build on God's grace, guidance and instructions. "And indeed We will make them taste of the Penalty of this (life) prior to the supreme Penalty, in order that they may (repent and) return" (Quran 32.21).

Sometimes hardship reminds us of God's enormous bounty. After all, do not the sick develop special appreciation for health? "But if you add up the favors of God, never will you be able to count them" (Quran 014.34). You begin to learn the value of things. Someone who has starved is more likely to give to the hungry and be generous and more of a comfort to those in trouble. It makes him more humble and grateful to God. It makes him turn to God and to develop trust in God. In short, he develops the attributes of those more likely to be raised in honor by God. Sahih Muslim book 32, number 6238: "'A'isha reported God's Messenger as saying: 'A believer does not receive (the trouble) of stepping on a thorn or more than that but God elevates him in rank or effaces his sins because of that."

While pain can come in many forms and from many sources, sometimes it comes from others who abuse you. Do not worry excessively, however if misfortune comes your way. Of course, there is normally nothing wrong with defending yourself against bad people. Remember also that God will compensate you for your misfortune if you are a pious servant of His. So do not worry too much. (Concentrate instead on pleasing God always). Do not forget that one of the names of God is Al-Muqsit, the Equitable, The One who is Just in His judgment.

Quran 5.27-29: Recite to them the truth of the story of the two sons of Adam. Behold! they each presented a sacrifice (to God). It was accepted from one, but not from the other. Said the latter: "Be sure I will kill you." "Surely," said the former, "God accepts the sacrifice of those who are righteous. If you raise your hand against me, to slay me, it is not for me to raises my hand against you to slay you for I do fear God, the Cherisher of the worlds. For me, I intend to let you draw on yourself my sin as well as yours, for you will be among the companions of the fire, and that is the reward of those who do wrong."

The following hadith explains these Quranic ayat (verses) better.

Sahih Muslim *book 32, number 6251:* Abu Huraira reported God's Messenger as saying: "Do you know who is poor?" They (the Companions of the Holy Prophet) said: "A poor man among us is one who has neither coins with him nor wealth." He (the Holy Prophet) said: "The poor one of my community would be he who would come on the Day of Resurrection with prayers and fasts and charitable acts, but (he would find himself bankrupt on that day as he would have exhausted his funds of virtues) because he hurled abuses upon others, brought calumny against others, unlawfully consumed the wealth of others and shed the blood of others and beat others, and his virtues would be credited to the account of one (who suffered at his hand). And if his good deeds fall short to clear the account, then his sins would be entered in (his account) and he would be thrown in the Hell-Fire."

Such is the "accounting" of the Day of Judgement. Everyone will be compensated in full and not wronged in the least.

Answer #3:

Sometimes calamity descends as a result of direct and arrogant rebellion against God.

Quran 29.38: "And (the fate of tribes of) A'ad and Thamud is manifest unto you from their (ruined and deserted) dwellings. Satan made their deeds seem fair unto them and so debarred them from the Way, though they were keen observers. And Korah, Pharaoh and Haman Moses came unto them with clear proofs (of God's Sovereignty), but they were boastful in the land. And they were not winners (in the race). So We took each one in his sin; of them was he on whom We sent a hurricane, and of them was he who was overtaken by the (Awful) Cry, and of them was he whom We caused the earth to swallow up, and of them was he whom We drowned. It was not for God to wrong them, but they wronged themselves.

Consider if God had not destroyed them. Consider if corruption and evil were allowed to reign supreme how severe the test would have been on anyone in that society who even would try to do good. But God is merciful to his servants.

Sometimes man expects God to listen to him but he does not listen to God. Where is the logic in this?

Sahih Muslim book 5, number 2214: Abu Huraira reported God's Messenger as saying: "O people, God is Good and He therefore accepts only that which is good. And God commanded the believers as He commanded the Messengers by saying:' O Messengers, eat of the good things, and do good deeds; verily I am aware of what you do'" (23 51). And He said: 'O those who believe, eat of the good things that We gave you' (2 172). He then spoke of a person who travels widely, his hair disheveled and covered with dust. He lifts his hand towards the sky (and thus makes the supplication): 'O Lord, O Lord,' whereas his diet is unlawful, his drink is unlawful, and his clothes are unlawful and his nourishment is unlawful. How then can his supplication be accepted?'"

Then there is this:

Narrated Anas ibn Malik: "God the Almighty told Ya'qoub (i.e. Jacob), through Jibreel: 'Do you know why I took your sight and bent your back, and why the brothers of Yusuf (i.e., Joseph) did what they did? You killed a sheep and a poor orphan who was fasting came by and you gave him nothing from it" (Al-Hakim).

Answer #4 (For Muslims in hardship)

Quran 2.214 Or do you think that you shall enter the Garden (of Bliss) without such (trials) as came to those who passed away before you? They encountered suffering and adversity, and were so shaken in spirit that even the Messenger and those of faith who were with him cried: "When (will come) the help of God." Ah! Verily, the help of God is (always) near!

Life can be a test. A difficult test. For those going through tough times, one of the primary causes of stress is worrying about one's capacity to handle a problem. Is the problem just too big for me? But a Muslim need not be worried on this account. God says in the Quran:

No soul shall have a burden laid on it greater than it can bear. (Quran 2.233).

and the following:

Sa'd asked the Prophet (peace and blessings of God be upon him): "O Messenger of God, which of the people suffers the most distress?" He said: "The Prophets, then those who come after them (in terms of status), then those who come after them. A man will be tested according to the strength of his faith. If his faith is strong, then the distress with which he is tried will be greater; if his faith is weak, he will be tested in accordance with the level of his faith. Distress will keep on befalling the servant until he walks on the face of the earth free from sin."

This means that everything dealt to you is within your capacity to handle Islamically. This in itself should be a source of great comfort. Also find comfort and tranquility in dhikr (remembrance of God). "In the remembrance of God do hearts find tranquility" (Quran 13:28).

One should also be careful not fall into the trap of despair which is a type of disbelief.

And who despairs of the Mercy of his Lord except those who are astray? [Quran 15:56]

The gravest of sins are to ... and to despair of the mercy of God" [1]

Also do not forget to count your blessings:

But if you add up the favors of God, never will you be able to number them (Quran 14.34)

If you are worried about having lost a leg consider the person who has lost two legs.

Sahih Muslim, book 42, number 7070: "Abu Huraira reported God's Messenger as saying: Look at those who stand at a lower level than you, but don't look at those who stand at a higher level, for this would make the favors (conferred upon you by God) insignificant (in your eyes)"

The companions of the prophet used to complain to the Prophet about the torture they were suffering...

Narrated Khabbab bin Al-Arat: "We complained to God's Apostle (of the persecution inflicted on us while he was sitting in the shade of the Kaaba, leaning over his Burd (i.e., covering sheet). We said to him, 'Would you seek help for us? Would you pray to God for us?' He said, 'Among the nations before you a (believing) man would be put in a ditch that was dug for him, and a saw would be put over his head and he would be cut into two pieces; yet that (torture) would not make him give up his religion. His body would be combed with iron combs that would remove his flesh from the bones and nerves, yet that would not make him abandon his religion. By God, this religion (i.e., Islam) will prevail until a traveler from Sana (in Yemen) to Hadramaut will fear none but God, or a wolf as regards his sheep, but you (people) are hasty'" (Bukhari 4.56.809).

A mu'mim (believer) is in a wonderful state. If good befalls him then he enjoys the good, if bad befalls him God uses it as a means to elevate him.

Sahih Bukhari, volume 7, book 70, number 545: Narrated Abu Sa'id Al-Khudri and Abu Huraira: The Prophet said, "No fatigue, nor disease, nor sorrow, nor sadness, nor hurt, nor distress befalls a Muslim, even if it were the prick he receives from a thorn, but that God expiates some of his sins for that."

Now consider the difficult case of a woman raped in the Bosnian concentration camps, consider the cases of Muslims being unjustly imprisoned, consider the case of unspeakable tortures being inflicted on individual Muslims who profess Islam, think of the worst most tragic, most grotesque miscarriage of justice of which you can think. Now consider not the worst case of just today's world but the worst case that has EVER(!) existed in the annals of time for mankind. What do you say about this one case? A case that stands as the epitome of seeming injustice. Herein lies the importance of understanding the differences between this world and the hereafter. Of weighing this world against the next. You see, God has put down a veil until the Day of Judgement when the realities of existence shall manifest themselves according to His command.

Sahih Muslim book 39, number 6738: Anas b. Malik reported that God's Messenger said that one among the denizens of Hell who had led a life of ease and plenty among the people of the world would be made to dip into the Fire only once on the Day of Resurrection and then it would be said to him: "O, son of Adam, did you find any comfort, did you happen to get any material blessing?" He would say: "By God, no, my Lord." And then that person from among the persons of the world would be brought who had led the most miserable life (in the world) from amongst the inmates of Paradise, and he would be made to dip once in Paradise and it would be said to him. "O, son of Adam, did you face, any hardship? Or had any distress fallen to your lot?" And he would say: "By God, no, O my Lord, never did I face any hardship or experience any distress."

Most certainly is our Lord al-'Adl (The Just) and al-Basir (The All-Seeing). All praise be to God, our Rabb, the Cherisher and Sustainer of the Worlds.

Sahih Muslim, book 4, number 2000: Umm Salama, the wife of the Apostle of God, reported God's Messenger as saying: "If any servant (of God) who suffers a calamity says: We belong to God and to Him shall we return; O God, reward me for my affliction and give me something better than it in exchange for it, God will give him reward for affliction, and will give him something better than it in exchange. She (Umm Salama) said: "When Abu Salama died, I uttered (these very words) as I was commanded (to do) by the Messenger of God. So God gave me better in exchange than him,. i. e., I was taken as the wife of) the Messenger of God.

When a Muslim feels despair and is on the verge of being overwhelmed by events, he should look to the example of our prophet. On one of the saddest days of his life, he was driven out, pelted by stones and bleeding, from Taif when he had tried to present Islam to them. Seeking refuge in an orchard, exhausted and greatly grieved, he said something from which we Muslims can learn much. He said, in this period of great anguish:

"O God! To You alone I make complaint of my helplessness, the paucity of my resources and my insignificance before mankind. You are the most Merciful of the mercifuls. You are the Lord of the helpless and the weak, O Lord of mine! Into whose hands would You abandon me: into the hands of an unsympathetic distant relative who would sullenly frown at me, or to the enemy who has been given control over my affairs? But if Your wrath does not fall on me, there is nothing for me to worry about." "I seek protection in the light of Your Countenance, which illuminates the heavens and dispels darkness, and which controls all affairs in this world as well as in the Hereafter. May it never be that I should incur Your wrath, or that You should be wrathful to me. And there is no power nor resource, but Yours alone."

We should remember that a pious Muslim's immediate concern is whether he has angered His Lord, but if this is not the case he turns to His Lord in recognition of the true reality of affairs. For he realizes that God is the source of *all* strength and power. He remembers His Grace and asks for His Mercy. And he knows that if his Lord is not unhappy with him he has nothing to fear.

Finally, the intelligent servant of God uses the hardship as a reminder to turn to God, but be not among those who are forgetful or ungrateful and forget God when God removes the hardship from them. Remember God in hardship and ease.

Quran 10:22-23: He it is Who enables you to traverse through land and sea; so that you even board ships; they sail in them with a favourable wind, and they rejoice at this; then comes a stormy wind and the waves come to them from all sides, and they think they are being overwhelmed: they cry unto God, sincerely offering (their) duty unto Him saying, "If You deliver us from this, we shall truly show our gratitude!" But when He delivers them, behold! they transgress insolently through the earth in defiance of right! O mankind! your insolence is against your own souls, an enjoyment of the life of the present: in the end, to Us is your return, and We shall show you the truth of all that you did."

Remember God in hardship and ease.

Note: Now a note about "fatalism," a term that reeks of many negative connotations that some elements have tried to associate with it. Islam does not advocate "fatalism," which implies laziness. In reality, anyone who has tried to strive in the way of God knows it is the opposite of laziness. But, if God has decreed something and one *truly* has no control over it, a Muslim does not waste time getting upset or stressed out about it.

These are just a few possible answers and of course, as always, only God truly knows the full answers best.

Endnotes
[1] Said by Ibn Masood, reported by Abd al-Razzaaq and classified as sahih by al-Haythami and Ibn Katheer.

The Quran & Modern Science

By Dr. Zakir Naik

Compiler's Note: "Quran & Modern Science" is the author's attempt to decipher and interpret certain verses in the Quran in light of currently available modern science. Due to space limitations, this is an abridged version of Dr. Naik's original booklet.

The Qur'an is not a book of science but a book of "signs," (i.e., Arabic: ayat or English translation:verses or signs). There are more than six thousand "signs" in the Qur'an. We all know that many times science takes a "U-turn." In this book I have considered only established scientific facts and not mere hypotheses and theories that are based on assumptions and are not backed by proof.

Chapter 5

ASTRONOMY

CREATION OF THE UNIVERSE: "THE BIG BANG"

The creation of the universe is explained by astrophysicists in a widely accepted phenomenon, popularly known as the "Big Bang." It is supported by observational and experimental data gathered by astronomers and astrophysicists for decades. According to the "Big Bang," the whole universe was initially one big mass. Then there was a "Big Bang" which resulted in the formation of galaxies. These then divided to form stars, planets, the sun, the moon, etc. The Qur'an contains the following verse, regarding the origin of the universe:

Do not the Unbelievers see that the heavens and the earth were joined together (as one Unit of Creation), before We clove them asunder? (Al-Qur'an 21:30)

An interesting similarity between the Qur'anic verse and the "Big Bang"?

INITIAL GASEOUS MASS BEFORE CREATION OF GALAXIES

Scientists agree that before the galaxies in the universe were formed, celestial matter was initially in the form of gaseous matter. In short, huge gaseous matter or clouds were present before the formation of the galaxies. To describe initial celestial matter, the word "smoke" is more appropriate than gas. The following Qur'anic verse refers to this state of the universe by the word *dhukhan* which means smoke.

Moreover, He comprehended In His design the sky, and it had been (as) smoke: He said to it and to the earth: "Come together, willingly or unwillingly." They said: "We do come (together), in willing obedience." (Al-Qur'an 41:11).

Again, this fact is a corollary to the "Big Bang" and was not known to anyone before the prophethood of Muhammad (peace be upon him)[1]. What then, could have been the source of this knowledge?

SHAPE OF THE EARTH IS SPHERICAL

In early times, people believed that the earth was flat. For centuries, men were afraid to venture out too far, for fear of falling off the edge! Sir Francis Drake was the first person who proved that the earth is spherical when he sailed around it in 1597. The earth is not exactly round like a ball, but geo-spherical, i.e., it is flattened at the poles. The following verse contains a description of the earth's shape: "And the earth, moreover, He has made egg shaped." [Al-Qur'an 79:30][2]

The Arabic word for egg here is *dahaahaa*, which means an ostrich egg. The shape of an ostrich egg resembles the geo-spherical shape of the earth. Thus the Qur'an correctly describes the shape of the earth, though the prevalent notion when the Qur'an was revealed was that the earth was flat.

MOONLIGHT IS REFLECTED LIGHT

It was believed by earlier civilizations that the moon

emits its own light. Science now tells us that the light of the moon is reflected light. This fact, however, was mentioned in the Qur'an 1,400 years ago in the following verse:

Blessed is He Who made Constellations in the skies and placed therein a Lamp and a Moon giving light (Al-Qur'an 25:61)

The Arabic word in the Qur'an, for the sun is *shams*. It is also referred to as *siraaj*, which means a "torch" or as *wahhaaj* meaning "a blazing lamp" or as *diya* which means "shining glory." All three descriptions are appropriate to the sun, since it generates intense heat and light by its internal combustion. The Arabic word for the moon is *qamar*, and it is described in the Qur'an as *muneer*, which is a body that gives *noor* i.e., reflected light. Again, the Qur'anic description matches perfectly with the true nature of the moon, which does not give off light by itself and is an inactive body that reflects the light of the sun. Not once in the Qur'an is the moon mentioned as *siraj*, *wahhaj* or *diya* or the sun as *noor* or *muneer*. This implies that the Qur'an recognizes the difference between the nature of sunlight and moonlight.

The following verses relate to the nature of light from the sun and the moon:

It is He who made the sun to be a shining glory and the moon to be a light (of beauty). [Al-Qur'an 10:5]

Do you not see how Allah has created the seven heavens one above another, and made the moon a light in their midst, and made the sun as a (glorious) lamp? [Al-Qur'an 71:15-16] .

THE SUN ROTATES

For a long time European philosophers and scientists believed that the earth stood still in the center of the universe and every other body including the sun moved around it. In the West, this geocentric concept of the universe was prevalent right from the time of Ptolemy in the second century B.C. In 1512, Nicholas Copernicus put forward his Heliocentric Theory of Planetary Motion, which asserted that the sun is motionless at the center of the solar system with the planets revolving around it.

In 1609, the German scientist Yohannus Keppler published the "Astronomia Nova." In this he concluded that the planets not only move in elliptical orbits around the sun, but rotate upon their axes at irregular speeds. With this knowledge it became possible for European scientists to explain correctly many of the mechanisms of the solar system, including the sequence of night and day.

After these discoveries, it was thought that the Sun was stationary and did not rotate about its axis like the Earth. I remember having studied this fallacy from geography books during my school days. Consider the following Qur'anic verse:

It is He Who created the night and the day, and the sun and the moon; all (the celestial bodies) swim along, each in its rounded course (Al-Qur'an 21:33).

The Arabic word used in the above verse is *yasbahoon*. The word is derived from the word *sabaha*. It carries with it the idea of motion that comes from any moving body. If you use the word for a person on the ground, it would not mean that he is rolling but would mean he is walking or running. If you use the word for a man in water it would not mean that he is floating but would mean that he is swimming.

Similarly, if you use the word *yasbah* for a celestial body such as the sun it would not mean that it is only flying through space but would mean that it is also rotating as it goes through space. Most of the school textbooks have incorporated the fact that the sun rotates about its axis. The rotation of the sun about its own axis can be proved with the help of equipment that projects the image of the sun on top of a table so that one can examine the image of the sun without being blinded. It is noticed that the sun has spots which complete a circular motion once every 25 days, i.e., the sun takes approximately 25 days to rotate around its axis.

The sun travels through space at roughly 240 km per second and takes about 200 million years to complete one revolution around the center of our Milky Way Galaxy.

It is not permitted for the sun to catch up with the moon, nor can the night outstrip the day; each (just) swims along in (its own) orbit (according to law) (Al-Qur'an 36:40).

This verse mentions an essential fact discovered by modern astronomy, i.e., the existence of the individual orbits of the Sun and the Moon, and their journey through space with their own motion.

The solar system is moving in space towards a point situated in the constellation of Hercules (Alpha Lyrae) .

The moon rotates around its axis in the same duration that it takes to revolve around the earth. It takes approximately 29½ days to complete one rotation. Should we not ponder over the question: "What was the source of knowledge contained in the Qur'an?"

THE SUN WILL BE EXTINGUISHED

The light of the sun is due to a chemical process on its surface that has been taking place continuously for the past five billion years. It will come to an end at some point of time in the future when the sun will be totally extinguished, leading to extinction of all life on earth. Regarding the impermanence of the sun's existence the Qur'an says:

> And the sun runs its course for a period determined for it; that is the decree of (Him) the exalted in Might, the All-Knowing (Al-Qur'an 36:38) [3].

The Arabic word used here is *mustaqarr*, which means a place or time that is determined. Thus the Qur'an says that the sun runs toward a determined place and will do so only up to a pre-determined period of time – meaning that it will end or be extinguished.

THE EXPANDING UNIVERSE

In 1925, American astronomer Edwin Hubble, provided observational evidence that all galaxies are moving away from one another, which implies that the universe is expanding. The expansion of the universe is now an established scientific fact. This is what Al-Qur'an says regarding the nature of the universe:

> With power and skill did We construct the Firmament for it is We Who create the vastness of space (Al-Qur'an 51:47)

The Arabic word *musioon* is correctly translated as "expanding it," and it refers to the creation of the expanding vastness of the universe. One of the greatest astrophysicists, Stephen Hawking, in his book, *A Brief History of Time*, says, "The discovery that the universe is expanding was one of the great intellectual revolutions of the 20th century."

The Qur'an mentioned the expansion of the universe, before man even learned to build a telescope! Some may say that the presence of astronomical facts in the Qur'an is not surprising since the Arabs were advanced in the field of astronomy. They are correct in acknowledging the advancement of the Arabs in the field of astronomy. They fail to realize however that the Qur'an was revealed centuries before the Arabs excelled in astronomy. Moreover, many of the scientific facts mentioned above regarding astronomy, such as the origin of the universe with a Big Bang, were not known to the Arabs even at the peak of their scientific advancement. The scientific facts mentioned in the Qur'an are therefore not due to the Arabs' advancement in astronomy. Indeed, the reverse is true. The Arabs advanced in astronomy, because astronomy occupies a place in the Qur'an.

PHYSICS

ATOMS CAN BE DIVIDED

In ancient times a well-known theory by the name of "Atomism" was widely accepted. This theory was originally proposed by the Greeks, in particular by a scholar called Democritus, who lived about 23 centuries ago. Democritus and the people that came after him assumed that the smallest unit of matter was the atom. The ancient Arabs used to believe the same. The Arabic word *zarrah* most commonly meant an atom. In recent times modern science has discovered that it is possible to split even an atom. That the atom can be split further is a development of the 20th century. Fourteen centuries ago this concept would have appeared unusual even to an Arab. For him the *zarrah* was the limit beyond which one could not go. The following Qur'anic verse, however, refuses to acknowledge this limit:

> The Unbelievers say, 'Never to us will come The Hour'; Say, "Nay! But most surely, by my Lord, it will come upon you – by Him Who knows the unseen from Whom is not hidden the least little atom in the Heavens or on earth; nor is there anything less than that, or greater, but is in the Record Perspicuous" (Al-Qur'an 34:3). [4]

This verse refers to the Omniscience of God, His knowledge of all things, hidden or apparent. It then goes further and says that God is aware of everything, including what is smaller or bigger than the atom. Thus the verse clearly shows that it is possible for something smaller than the atom to exist, a fact discovered only recently by modern science.

OCEANOLOGY

BARRIER BETWEEN SWEET AND SALT WATERS

> He has let free the two bodies of flowing water, meeting together: between them is a barrier that they do not transgress (Al-Qur'an 55:19-20).

In the Arabic text the word *barzakh* means a barrier or a partition. This barrier, however, is not a physical partition. The Arabic word *maraja* literally means "they both meet and mix with each other." Early commentators of the Qur'an were unable to explain the two opposite meanings for the two bodies of water, i.e. they meet and mix, and at the same time, there is a barrier between them. Modern Science has discovered that in the places where two different seas meet, there is a barrier between them. This barrier divides the two seas so that each sea has its own temperature, salinity and density. [5] Oceanologists are now in a better position to explain this verse. There is a slanted unseen water barrier between the two seas through which water from one sea passes to the other.

But, when the water from one sea enters the other sea, it loses its distinctive characteristic and becomes homogenized with the other water. In a way this barrier serves as a transitional homogenizing area for the two waters. This phenomenon is also mentioned in the following verse of the Qu'ran:

And made a separating bar between the two bodies of flowing water? (Al-Qur'an 27:61])

This phenomenon occurs in several places, including the divider between the Mediterranean and the Atlantic Ocean at Gibraltar. A white bar can also be clearly seen at Cape Point, Cape Peninsula, South Africa, where the Atlantic Ocean meets the Indian Ocean.

But when the Qur'an speaks about the divider between fresh and salt water, it mentions the existence of "a forbidding partition" with the barrier.

It is He Who has let free the two bodies of flowing water, one palatable and sweet, and the other salty and bitter; yet He has made a barrier between them, and a partition that is forbidden to be passed (Al-Qur'an 25:53).

Modern science has discovered that in estuaries, where fresh (sweet) and salt-water meet, the situation is somewhat different from that found in places where two salt water seas meet. It has been discovered that what distinguishes fresh water from salt water in estuaries is a "pycnocline zone with a marked density discontinuity separating the two layers." [6] This partition (zone of separation) has salinity different from both the fresh water and the salt water. [7]

This phenomenon occurs in several places, including Egypt, where the river Nile flows into the Mediterranean Sea.

ZOOLOGY

THE BEE AND ITS SKILL

> And your Lord taught the bee to build its cells in hills,
> on trees, and in (men's) habitations, then to eat of all the
> produce (of the earth), and find with skill the spacious
> paths of its Lord (Al-Qur'an 16:68-69)

Von-Frisch received the Nobel Prize in 1973 for his
research on the behaviour and communication of
bees. The bee, after discovering any new garden or
flower, goes back and tells its fellow bees the exact
direction and map to get there, which is known as
"bee dance." The meanings of this insect's movements
that are intended to transmit information between
worker bees have been discovered scientifically
using photography and other methods. The Qur'an
mentions in the above verse how the bee finds with
skill the spacious paths of its Lord.

The gender used for the bee is the female gender
(*fa'slukî* and *kulî*), indicating that the bee that leaves
its home for gathering food is a female bee. In other
words the soldier or worker bee is a female bee. In
fact, in Shakespeare's play, "Henry the Fourth," some
of the characters speak about bees and mention that
the bees are soldiers and that they have a king. That
is what people thought in Shakespearean times.
They thought that the worker bees are male bees and
they go home and are answerable to a king bee. This,
however, is not true. The worker bees are females

and they do not report to a king bee but to a queen bee. But it took modern investigations in the last 300 years to discover this.

LIFESTYLE AND COMMUNICATION OF ANTS

Consider the following Qur'anic verse:

> And before Solomon were marshaled his hosts – of jinns and men and birds, and they were all kept in order and ranks. At length, when they came to a (lowly) valley of ants, one of the ants said: 'O you ants, get into your habitations, lest Solomon and his hosts crush you (under foot) without knowing it" (Al-Qur'an 27:17-18).

In the past, some people probably would have mocked at the Qur'an, taking it to be a fairy tale book in which ants talk to each other and communicate sophisticated messages. In recent times, research has shown us several facts about the lifestyle of ants, which were not known earlier to humankind. Research has shown that the animals or insects whose lifestyle is closest in resemblance to the lifestyle of human beings are the ants. This can be seen from the following findings regarding ants:

a.   The ants bury their dead in a manner similar to humans.

b.   They have a sophisticated system of division of labour, whereby they have managers, supervisors, foremen, workers, etc.

c.   Once in a while they meet among themselves to have a "chat."

d. They have an advanced method of communication among themselves.

e. They hold regular "markets" where they exchange goods.

f. They store grains for long periods in winter and, if the grain begins to bud, they cut the roots, as if they understand that if they leave it to grow, it will rot. If the grains stored by them get wet due to rains, they take these grains out into the sunlight to dry, and, once these are dry, they take them back inside as though they know that humidity will cause development of root systems and thereafter rotting of the grain.

MEDICINE

HONEY: HEALING FOR HUMANKIND

The bee assimilates juices of various kinds of flowers and fruit and forms honey within its body, which it stores in its cells of wax. Only a couple of centuries ago man came to know that honey comes from the belly of the bee. This fact was mentioned in the Qur'an 1,400 years ago in the following verse:

> There issues from within their bodies a drink of varying colours, wherein is healing for men (Al-Qur'an 16:69).

We are now aware that honey has a healing property and also a mild antiseptic property. The Russians used honey to cover their wounds in World War II. The wound would retain moisture and would leave very little scar tissue. Due to the density of honey, no fungus or bacteria would grow in the wound. Dramatic improvements were visible in 22 incurable chest and Alzheimer's disease patients at nursing homes in England who were treated by Sister Carole, a nun, with propolis, a substance that bees produce to seal hives against bacteria. [8]

A person suffering from an allergy of a particular plant may be given honey from that plant so that the person develops resistance to that allergy. Honey is also rich in fructose and vitamin K. Thus the knowledge contained in the Qur'an regarding honey, its origin and properties, was discovered centuries after its revelation.

EMBRYOLOGY

MUSLIMS SEEK ANSWERS

A group of Muslim scholars, under the direction of an eminent Yemani scholar, Sheikh Abdul Majid Azzindani, collected information concerning embryology [9] and other sciences in the Qur'an and undisputed Hadith [10] and translated it into English. They then followed the Qur'anic advice:

If you do not realise this ask of those who possess the Message (Al-Qur'an 16:43 & 21:7).

All the information from the Qur'an and the undisputed Hadith concerning embryology was gathered, translated into English, and presented to Prof. (Dr.) Keith Moore, who was Professor of

Embryology and Chairman of the Department of Anatomy at the University of Toronto in Canada. At present he is one of the highest authorities in the field of embryology.

He was asked to give his opinion regarding the material presented to him. After carefully examining it, Dr. Moore said that most of the information concerning embryology mentioned in the Qur'an and the undisputed Hadith is in perfect conformity with modern discoveries in the field of embryology and does not conflict with them in any way. He added that there were a few verses however, on whose scientific accuracy he could not comment. He could not say whether the statements were true or false, since he was himself unaware of the information contained therein. There was also no mention of this information in modern writings and studies on embryology.

One such verse is:

Proclaim! (or Read!) In the name of your Lord and Cherisher, Who created – created man, out of a (mere) clot of congealed blood (Al-Qur'an 96:1-2)

The Arabic word *alaq* besides meaning a congealed clot of blood also means something that clings, a leech-like substance. Dr. Keith Moore had no knowledge whether an embryo in the initial stages appears like a leech. To check this out he studied the initial stage of the embryo under a very powerful microscope in his laboratory and compared what he observed with a diagram of a leech. He was astonished at the striking resemblance between the two!

In the same manner, he acquired more information on embryology from the Qur'an that was hitherto not known to him, Dr. Keith Moore answered about eighty questions dealing with embryological data mentioned in the Qur'an and Hadith. Noting that the information contained in the Qur'an and Hadith was in full agreement with the latest discoveries in the field of embryology, Prof. Moore said, "If I were asked these questions thirty years ago, I would not have been able to answer half of them for lack of scientific information."

In 1981, during the Seventh Medical Conference in Dammam, Saudi Arabia, Dr. Moore said, "It has been a great pleasure for me to help clarify statements in the Qur'an about human development. It is clear to me that these statements must have come to Muhammad from God or Allah, because almost all of this knowledge was not discovered until many centuries later. This proves to me that Muhammad must have been a messenger of God or Allah." [11]

Dr. Keith Moore had earlier authored the book, *The Developing Human*. In 1982, after acquiring new knowledge from the Qur'an, he wrote, the 3rd edition of the same book, The book was the recipient of an award for the best medical book written by a single author. This book has been translated into several major languages of the world and is used as a textbook of embryology in the first year of medical studies.

Dr. Joe Leigh Simpson, Chairman of the Department of Obstetrics and Gynecology, at the Baylor College of Medicine, Houston, Texas proclaims: "these Hadiths, sayings of Muhammad could not have been obtained on the basis of the scientific knowledge that was available at the time of the writer (7th century). It follows that not only is there no conflict between genetics and religion (Islam) but in fact religion (Islam) may guide science by adding revelation to some of the traditional scientific approaches ... There exist statements in the Qur'an shown centuries later to be valid that support knowledge in the Qur'an having been derived from God."

SEX DETERMINATION

The sex of a foetus is determined by the nature of the sperm and not of the ovum. The sex of the child, whether female or male, depends on whether the 23rd pair of chromosomes is XX or XY respectively. Primarily, sex determination occurs at fertilization and depends upon the type of sex chromosome in the sperm that fertilizes an ovum. If it is an "X" bearing sperm that fertilizes the ovum, the foetus is a female and if it is a "Y" bearing sperm then the foetus is a male.

That He did create in pairs – male and female, from a seed when lodged (in its place) (Al-Qur'an 53:45-46)

The Arabic word *nutfah* means a minute quantity of liquid and *tumnaa* means ejaculated or planted.

Therefore nutfah specifically refers to sperm because

it is ejaculated. The Qur'an says:

> Was he not a drop of sperm emitted (In lowly form)? ... Then did he become a clinging clot; then did (Allah) make and fashion (him) in due proportion. ... and of him He made two sexes, male and female." [Al-Qur'an 75:37-39]

Here again it is mentioned that a small quantity (drop) of sperm (indicated by the word *nutfatan min maniyyin*) which comes from the man is responsible for the sex of the fetus.

FOETUS PROTECTED BY THREE VEILS OF DARKNESS

> He makes you, in the wombs of your mothers, in stages, one after another, in three veils of darkness (Al-Qur'an 39:6)

According to Prof. Keith Moore these three veils of darkness in the Qur'an refer to:

1). the anterior abdominal wall of the mother

2) the uterine wall

3) the amnio-chorionic membrane.

EMBRYONIC STAGES

> Man We did create from a quintessence (of clay); then We placed him as (a drop of) sperm in a place of rest, firmly fixed; then We made the sperm into a clot of

congealed blood; then of that clot We made a (foetus) lump; then We made out of that lump bones and clothed the bones with flesh; then We developed out of it another creature. So blessed be Allah, The Best to create! (Al-Qur'an 23:12-14)

In this verse Allah states that man is created from a small quantity of liquid which is placed in a place of rest, firmly fixed (well established or lodged) for which the Arabic word *qaraarin makeen* is used.

The uterus is well protected from the posterior by the spinal column supported firmly by the back muscles. The embryo is further protected by the amniotic sac containing the amniotic fluid. Thus the foetus has a well protected dwelling place.

This small quantity of fluid is made into *alaqah*, meaning something which clings. It also means a leech-like substance. Both descriptions are scientifically acceptable as in the very early stages the foetus clings to the wall and also appears to resemble the leech in shape. It also behaves like a leech (blood sucker) and acquires its blood supply from the mother through the placenta. The third meaning of the word *alaqah* is a blood clot. During this alaqah stage, which spans the third and fourth week of pregnancy, the blood clots within closed vessels. Hence the embryo acquires the appearance of a blood clot in addition to acquiring the appearance of a leech. Compare the readily available Qur'anic knowledge with the struggle over scientific findings:

In 1677, Hamm and Leeuwenhoek were the first scientists to observe human sperm cells (spermatozoa) through a microscope. They thought that a sperm cell contained a miniature human being which grew in the uterus to form a newborn. This was known as the perforation theory. When scientists discovered that the ovum was bigger than the sperm, it was thought by De Graf and others that the foetus existed in a miniature form in the ovum. Later, in the 18th century Maupertuis propagated the theory of biparental inheritance.

The *alaqah* is transformed into *mudghah* which means "something that is chewed (having teeth marks)" and also something that is tacky and small which can be put in the mouth like gum. Both these explanations are scientifically correct. Prof. Keith Moore took a piece of plaster seal and made it into the size and shape of the early stage of foetus and chewed it between the teeth to make it into a "*mudghah.*" He compared this with the photographs of the early stage of a foetus. The teeth marks resembled the "somites" which is the early formation of the spinal column. This *mudghah* is transformed into bones (*izām*). The bones are clothed with intact flesh or muscles (*lahm*). Then Allah makes it into another creature.

Prof. Marshall Johnson who is one of the leading scientists in the United States, and is the head of the Department of Anatomy and Director of the Daniel Institute at the Thomas Jefferson University in Philadelphia, was asked to comment on the verses of the Qur'an dealing with embryology. At first, he said that the verses of the Qur'an describing the embryological stages cannot be a coincidence. It was probable that Muhammad had a powerful microscope. On being reminded that the Qur'an was revealed 1400 years ago and microscopes were invented many centuries after the time of Prophet Muhammad, Prof. Johnson laughed and admitted that the first microscope invented could not magnify more than 10 times and could not show a clear picture.

Later he said: "I see nothing here in conflict with the concept that Divine intervention was involved when Muhammad recited the Qur'an." [12]

According to Dr. Keith Moore, the modern classification of embryonic development stages, which is adopted throughout the world, is not easily comprehensible, since it identifies stages on a numerical basis, i.e., stage I, stage II, etc. On the other hand, the divisions revealed in the Qur'an are based on distinct and easily identifiable forms or shapes, which the embryo passes through. These are based on different phases of prenatal development and provide elegant scientific descriptions that are comprehensible and practical. Embryological stages of human development have been described in the following verses:

Was he not a drop of sperm emitted (in lowly form)? Then did he become a clinging clot; then did (Allah) make and fashion (him) in due proportion. And of him He made two sexes, male and female (Al-Qur'an 75:37-39]).

...Him Who created you, fashioned you in due proportion, and gave you a just bias; in whatever form He wills, does He put you together (Al-Qur'an 82:7-8).

EMBRYO PARTLY FORMED AND PARTLY UNFORMED

At the *muqdhah* stage, if an incision is made in the embryo and the internal organs are dissected, it will be seen that most of them are formed while the others are not yet completely formed.

According to Prof. Johnson, if we describe the embryo as a complete creation, then we are only describing that part which is already created. If we describe it as an incomplete creation, then we are only describing that part which is not yet created. So, is it a complete creation or an incomplete creation? There is no better description of this stage of embryogenesis than the Qur'anic description, "partly formed and partly unformed," as in the following verse:

> We created you out of dust, then out of sperm, then out of a leech-like clot, then out of a morsel of flesh, partly formed and partly unformed, so that We may manifest (Our power) to you. (Al-Qur'an 22:5).

Scientifically we know that at this early stage of development there are some cells that are differentiated and there are some cells that are undifferentiated – some organs are formed and yet others unformed.

CONCLUSION

To attribute the presence of scientific facts in the Qur'an to coincidence would be against common sense and a true scientific approach. Indeed the scientific accuracy of the Qur'anic verses confirm the Qur'an's open declaration.

Soon will We show them Our Signs in the (furthest) regions (of the earth), and in their own souls, until it becomes manifest to them that this is the Truth. Is it not enough that your Lord does witness all things?" [Al-Qur'an 41:53]

The Qur'an invites all humans to reflect on the Creation of the universe in the verse:

Behold! In the creation of the heavens and the earth, and the alternation of night and day – there are indeed signs for men of understanding (Al-Qur'an 3:190]

Endnotes

[1] Muslims also send salutations upon all the previously divinely inspired prophets on taking their names.

[2] The Arabic word dahaha has been translated by A. Yusuf Ali as "vast expanse," which also is correct. The word also means an ostrich egg.

[3] A similar message is conveyed in the Qur'an in 13:2, 35:13, 39:5 and 39:21.

[4] A similar message is conveyed in the Qur'an in 10:61.

[5] *Principles of Oceanography*, Davis, pp. 92-93.

[6] Oceanography, Gross, p. 242. Also see *Introductory*

Oceanography, Thurman, pp. 300-301.

[7] *Oceanography,* Gross, p. 244 and *Introductory Oceanography,* Thurman, pp. 300-301.

[8] The reference for this statement is the video tape entitled "This is the Truth" For a copy of this video contact the Islamic Research Foundation.

[9] Embryology is the study of human development before birth.

[10] Hadith or Sunnah means the sayings or actions of Prophet Muhammad.

[11] The reference for this statement is the video tape entitled "This is the Truth." For a copy of this video tape contact the Islamic Research Foundation.

[12] The reference for this statement is the video tape titled "This is the Truth." For a copy of this video tape contact the Islamic Research Foundation.

Disclaimer: This article and this book do not provide medical advice. Please see a doctor if you are not well.

Compiler's note: While Muslims acknowledge that the Quran contains scientific and other miracles it does not form the core of their belief system. The primary source of a Muslim's belief centers around practicing the Quran and the Sunnah. Due to the nature of scientific inquiry, scientific theories can and do undergo oscillating paradigm shifts. Important models are discarded, theories are refined, new ideas are born. Thus, even this chapter would have to be periodically rewritten, even as a core set of methodologies could remain intact.   Eventually, Muslims would expect improved data, deeper scientific understanding and Quranic interpretations to align themselves.

Why I Believe in God — A Muslim Speaks

By F. Kamal

REASON #1

Why do we exist? The argument of random evolution cannot be satisfying for the thoughtful individual. If we analyze the probability of our ordered world forming purely by chance, the probabilities are just too infinitesimally low. There are so many variables that must coincide – some with very low degrees of tolerance for "error." Moreover the laws of statistics themselves function to make the assumption of pure chance less appealing. For example, the likelihood of two coin flips being tails is $\frac{1}{2} \times \frac{1}{2} = \frac{1}{4}$, of three coin flips $\frac{1}{2} \times \frac{1}{2} \times \frac{1}{2} = \frac{1}{8}$, and of four coin flips $\frac{1}{2} \times \frac{1}{2} \times \frac{1}{2} \times \frac{1}{2} = \frac{1}{16}$ and so on. Notice how rapidly the likelihood decreases by increasing the number of events. Yet for us to exist, we depend on the optimal confluence of so many, many events. For example, the distance between the earth and the sun is on average 93 million miles from the sun. This is just the right distance to support life. If the earth had been just slightly closer all life would have perished from the heat, slightly further and we would have all frozen. While the earth's rotation allows us to enjoy 24 hour days – there is no reason that, had things been different, and the earth's rotation slower, each individual night could not have stretched for many, many months. This effect alone would eradicate most, if not all, life on earth. Nor is there any reason that the earth's rotation around the sun should be 365.2422 days. If instead, winters alone lasted 43 years—for example, life would have a hard time establishing itself. If our atmosphere were made of hydrogen, helium, methane, and ammonia (as is, for example, the atmosphere on Jupiter) without the requisite amount of oxygen, life on earth would perish. If water did not exist with different properties as a liquid, gas, and solid, how would the water cycle and current flows replenish and recycle the important ecological and nutritional cycles maintaining the web of life. Without a protective earthly atmosphere life would be vulnerable to meteors, sharp temperature fluctuations, cosmic/uv rays—all threatening life in their own way. And we have only mentioned a few environmental variables. If we were to consider, for example, the existence of something as extraordinarily complex as an animal, the probabilities would again plummet.

For argument's sake, let us consider humans. In order to describe the extraordinary structure that is a human, let us structurally decompose a human into modular functions/parts. Even then a simple module like walking itself turns out to be extremely complex. Computer and robotic labs in modern advanced universities with some of the smartest people in the world, using different algorithms, robots and artificial intelligence had labored for years to master this and other simple biological functions. (Yet a spider does it so easily.) How likely is it that a PhD student in a robotics lab could just randomly roll together random parts and arbitrary combinations to form a functional robot? How about if he or she used a random letter generator to write the code for a functional artificial intelligence program? (We are talking about probabilities well, well below 1% here). And we just mentioned walking. How about running, jumping, talking, listening, etc., etc.

Scientists have even worked for several years on enhancing an "artificial nose." This contrasts with the elegant power and sophisticated precision of bloodhounds and parasitic wasps. How about all the other senses?

The probabilities fall so rapidly. We have not even discussed the building of a heart, kidney or brain. If we look at biological processes at the molecular level of biochemistry, we see huge numbers of exquisitely precision-tooled processes acting with extraordinary synchronization and sequencing. We have highlighted a very limited number of variables to flush out the gist of the argument, and yet the combined probabilities have dropped so precipitously.

For by now, it should be obvious to the reader that there are millions and millions of factors that this line of reasoning could highlight, each factor further depressing the ultimate probabilities for life. While even if such events occurring purely by chance may be *possible*, it is simply not *probable*. So to cling to the notion that an event of infinitesimally low probability has taken place by chance is rather incredible. If a person is comfortable with odds like that, I am sure gamblers would be fighting with each other to meet this individual. (I can see it now: "You mean you're not willing to put your money where your mouth is?" "I tell you what, I'll give you trillion-to-one odds ..."). Yet it never fails to amaze me that individuals who would not gamble even a thousand dollars on insane (sorry... there really is no other word) odds, do so with God, without a second thought. [1]

Example #1: Consider if scientists were to discover an extraordinarily advanced empty spaceship during a probe of a planet or galaxy. How many scientists would explain its existence as a random dice roll by the universe? Would this be a mainstream, credible scientific explanation? What would happen if abandoned buildings and cities were discovered next? Would talk of an intelligent creator of these things be summarily dismissed by the scientific community?

Yet we see around us incongruous signs of objects and processes of extremely high organization. Who is the Creator?

REASON #2

While science offers much for man and should definitely be studied, its value should be kept in perspective. Science cannot become a god. Although science is extremely useful when used properly, if used alone or elevated to the status of a god, it can also be very unsatisfying for the truly probing mind. Science is used to answer what I would call

"How? Questions" not *"Who? Or Why? Questions."* While no one contests the value of answering *"How? Questions,"* raising science to a god and refusing to answer *"Why? Questions"* itself causes many problems. A certain narrow mindedness and blind myopia can thus result with people who take science as their god, relegating *"Why? Questions"* to, at best, a category of questions not worthy of being brought up. But if a mind is really thirsty for knowledge, it should ask if such disingenuous evasions suggest a selective use of intellect.

Science excels at answering *"How? Questions"* but is not always good in answering *"Why? Questions."* For example the science of mechanics and physics explain the How? of classical mechanics (by $F=MA$, $d=vt$, etc. for example) which is very useful for determining missile trajectories, etc. Yet *"Why?"* Do these "laws" hold? Alternatively, Big Bang can, with an initial mass and initial conditions, do a good job of explaining certain data (e.g. cosmic data), answering a good *"How? Question"* but completely abandoning the *"Why Question"* of why do the initial mass/energy/conditions exist?

If you read an engineering book on flying, it will say that the lift caused on the airplane wings is due to the Bernoulli principle. The airfoil curvature on takeoff causes the upper air to move faster then the lower air flow. This causes a pressure imbalance that provides lift to the plane. While this is a very good *"How? Question"* and answer, it does not explain *"Why?"* Bernoulli's principle exists in the first place. Why does a steel ship float? The answer by science is that the ship is primarily air (not steel, e.g. the inside of the ship). Since air has a lower density than water it rises to the top, because lower density items rise above higher density items. The upthrust on the ship is determined, according to Archimedes Principle, by the weight of the displaced water. It doesn't really answer the *"Why? Question"* but rather a *"How? Question."* The *"Why? Question"* is why does Archimedes Principle hold? Or, for that matter, why do different laws of thermodynamics and aerodynamics hold? You see, ultimately, observed phenomena are reduced to models and the functioning of such models to certain axioms and laws, but no explanation is offered for why these fundamental "laws," principles, equations, axioms, or whatever you want to call them, exist.

It could be argued that scientists do, over time, try to answer *"Why? Questions."* After all, models do evolve in response to new data. Classical Newtonian mechanics equations can evolve and can be retrofitted with their relativistic counterparts to deal with Einstein's theories, for example. New theories can be verified by new data. Empirical comparisons of ground and upper atmosphere muon intensities do suggest apparent increases in half-lives of the particles (relative time dilation) as predicted in Einstein's Theory of Special Relativity for particles traveling close to the speed of light.[2] Light can be shed on Newton's concept of gravity with the newer notions of gravitons and space-time warps in the world of astronomy.

These new formulations however, produce their own *"Why? Questions."* So, in a sense these advances really are answering *"How? Questions"*, not a certain class of "*Why? Questions.*" In a sense, these advances are giving more sophisticated answers to "*How? Questions.*" Depending on the sophistication of models, such models can evolve and have recursive like elements and/or themselves recursively become part of models. As model chains grow they may better answer how questions. Yet parts (such as some axioms and assumptions) escape the realm of the model's ability to explain. While chains of these models can be built, the chains are not all-encompassing, and there will be some part, axiom or assumption that remains unexplained by the current chain of models.

Or perhaps for those more literary minded this quote from Shakespeare's Hamlet:

There are more things in heaven and earth, Horatio,
Than are dreamt of in your philosophy.

At any rate, this approach, e.g. to carefully analyze "*How? Questions*" and ignore a class of ""*Who? And Why? Questions*", is so intellectually one-sided as to be obvious to even the uneducated and very young.

On a different note:

Writing this triggered a childhood recollection of mine. Since it was a long time ago the details may well be fuzzy, but the essence I remember very clearly.

When I was a child, an uncle shared with me a valuable lesson he had learnt. He told me how he had once become very angry with another relative of ours. This other person had for a short while, wielded a certain amount of economic influence in a poor, developing nation. My uncle felt that the policies enacted by this relative had harmed individuals, and had indignantly let him know that.

In response he was told a parable by that relative that went something like this:

You see someone sitting on high wall. Right below him another man is swinging his arms about wildly, drowning in a deep pool of water. You fully expect the man to jump in and rescue him, but to your disgust he leaps away out of sight to safety.

What a terrible man you think!

But what you did not know was that on the other side of that high wall was another pool with three women and their babies that were drowning, and that he had jumped in to save them.

I only recount this because it warns me how dimly one can sometimes perceive truth.

Truth sometimes is difficult to perceive, to tease out. Shining the light of examination even at a slightly different angle can reveal a completely different facet of the truth. But the truth may remain obscured since it may be difficult to extract and properly analyze 100% of the data. Science is a wonderful tool, and should be rigorously and responsibly pursued, but it can not be always be a perfect proxy for truth as it can take 180 degree U-turns as theories are refined and new data unearthed. Nor is there a complete guarantee that all the information that exists can be observed and processed by us.

(Perhaps in the same way that if one were living a two-dimensional world, one may never "see" three-dimensional cubes if they did not cross, or interact with, our plane of existence.)

REASON #3

How does one explain instinct? Science is content with relegating things it cannot currently answer temporarily to "black boxes" to be dealt with at a later time (hopefully when instruments become more powerful, etc.). Even if such mechanisms are unveiled in the future, such discoveries are sure to prompt awe at the magnificent inner working of the universe. There are some remarkable cases of instinct in nature. Perhaps one should not overlook, devalue or discount them. Should not one ask questions? How does a bird know how to build a nest or fly for the very first time, a mammal give birth without having done it before, young ones immediately upon birth know how to nourish themselves, a beaver build a (concave) dam? Who is "the ultimate programmer of this animal.?" And why does this code exist? (That is a "Why? Question" as opposed to the "How? Question," e.g. how does the program work?)

REASON #4

The beauty of the universe. The universe is not just functional, it is beautiful! It is difficult looking at a beautiful waterfall, gazing at a star-filled night, or walking through a forest to not believe that there is a

God. Does such extraordinary beauty just randomly appear? What artist could just walk away from his easel and brush and come back later and have his canvas filled with the most beautiful and heart-felt pictures by chance only? Not only is there beauty in the physical worlds, but also in the virtual worlds of mathematics and physics. What thinking scientist cannot marvel at the extraordinary elegance of so many laws governing so many seemingly complex and unrelated phenomena? Is there not some creative unseen Intelligence at work here? Muslims cannot help but stand in awe with each unfolding discovery of science as the Majesty of God's creation unfolds before them. "How great is the subtlety, elegance, beauty, and artistry of our Lord?", Muslims marvel.

Today's discoveries uncover worlds previously unknown, such as the worlds uncloaked by the electron microscope and strange and wonderful creatures discovered in the latest deep sea discoveries. The extraordinary, delicate, elegant connections in the web of ecology seem to be a testament to an extraordinary Creativity, Artistry, and Intelligence, not just random dice rolls [3] , behind our universe.

REASON #5

Let us assume for a moment that you do not believe in God, Heaven, Hell and the Day of Judgment. Consider this: What if God doesn't exist and you die without believing in God? Will you be jumping up and down with joy once you die? Hardly! Consider next what if God exists and you die without believing in God? Will you be jumping up and down with joy once you die? Hardly!

REASON #6

On a personal note, I feel I do see *some* signs of truth in the extraordinary impact of Islam on individuals, families, communities and the actual course of history. While I do not stress them, it would not be right to completely dismiss these signs without any thought. I do realize this is an area about which some may differ with me. I mention them, not at any length, but merely to give a flavor of them. For example, not too many forces in history have managed to transform some of their greatest enemies to their greatest defenders. Umar, for example, went from being a powerful persecutor of Islam and to almost killing the prophet Muhammad into one of the greatest Muslims and the 2nd Caliph (leader) of Islam.

The transformation of Malcolm X is also an interesting story. Here was an individual filled with great anger and resentment toward whites, who, after encountering Islam, was able to look beyound race for assessing his relationship with whites.

Malcolm X is not alone. Others have confronted environments of drugs, gangs, prostitution and crime and worse, and pulled themselves out of that morass. Islam has transformed the lives of so many lost individuals who then strive to do what is right. It can succeed where sometimes social spending, social engineering, and rehab programs cannot. Clearly, Islam touches something deep in the human soul.

It is also illustrative to read the stories of the companions of the Prophet and how he transformed a nation that buried alive its infant daughters, lived in a state of ignorance and immorality, worshipped idols, committed all sorts of abominations and shameful deeds, broke the ties of kinship, treated guests badly and the strong exploited the weak into a nation that soon after the advent of prophet Muhammad became a beacon for justice, truth and compassion. The impact of Muhammad on the entire course of history was so dramatic, so unprecedented, that even a non-Muslim, when writing a popular book ranking the 100 most influential people in human history choose to place him at the top of the list.

Not only was an entire new system of life brought to a motley, backward, ignoble people, but it transformed them so rapidly in a few years as to completely overtake and overpower the superpowers of the day: the mighty Persian and Byzantine Empires.

REASON #7

How can the "phenomenon of Muhammad" be explained? How can someone who was illiterate suddenly be associated with the Quran. The Quran has deep acoustical rhythms, literary merit, and wisdom. It is easily the pinnacle of the whole Arabic language. Yet Prophet Muhammad was illiterate. Also what motive would Muhammad have for his mission? His early years were punctuated by persecutions and sorrow. Some of his followers were brutally tortured and killed, some forced to migrate, his clan was boycotted, and he was even stoned by the children in the village of Ta'if. With endless misery and almost certain extermination in sight, what motive would there be to continue? Was the motive wealth, status or prestige? What was his motive? Yet even when the Quraish (his tribe) offered him great wealth and kingship if he abandoned his mission, he refused. On one occasion, he told his uncle, "By God if they put the sun in my right hand and the moon in my left on condition that I abandon this course, until God has made me victorious, or I perish therein, I would not abandon it." Not only is there difficulty in establishing motive but one must remember that the Prophet had established himself (long before his prophethood) as someone known for his honesty, fair dealings, truthfulness and trustworthiness. His character was impeccable. In fact the Quraish had conferred on him the title of Al-'Ameen (trustworthy).

REASON #8

While there are miracles associated with Prophet Muhammad. Muslims prefer to emphasize the miracle of the Quran. (Note: Muslims believe that the Quran is the exact word of God as revealed to Prophet Muhammad through Archangel Gabriel.) They prefer to emphasize the Quran because it is, in a sense, a "living miracle"; it can be read, recited, analyzed, and studied even today. It is clearly an acoustic miracle, a linguistic miracle, and a deep reservoir of wisdom. The Quran has an outstanding challenge for disbelievers to duplicate a similar work – but the challenge has not been answered in over 1400 years.

There are many aspects of the Quran that point

to its divine origin. For example in the Surah "The Byzantines," the Quran predicts the defeat of the Persians at the hands of the Byzantines. But these ayat (i.e. verses) were revealed at a time when the Byzantines had suffered several crushing and serious defeats at the hands of the Persians. It was only many years later, in a startling reversal of fate, that the Persians were in fact defeated "at the hands of the Byzantines." There are ayat (verses) in the Quran revealing facts about human embryology that were only recently discovered by modern science and could not possibly have been known 1400 years ago. This point becomes more poignant if one bothers to examine the tools and theories that existed during that time period. Much of what we take for granted today was very far from the way people used to think long ago.

In recent years, some Muslims have reexamined religious texts in light of modern science. What is interesting is that certain linguistic readings and new interpretations seem to concur with recent scientific discoveries. What makes it interesting is that the Quran was revealed 1400 years ago, long before these discoveries were made. Is this mere coincidence? Is there any validity to these interpretations? And if so, how could this information have been known? Or is one reading too much into these interpretations? Regardless of how one may feel about some of these interpretations, they can sometimes make for interesting reading.

For example do Quranic verses allude to the fact that the earth was round? [4] Some verses in the Quran seem to point to this.

Also interesting are the recent analysis of certain Quranic words and verses that point toward the fact that the moon is not the source of its own light, but rather reflected light, something only recently discovered by science. There are many aspects to the Quran that challenge the notion of the Quran being man-made, only a few of which have been mentioned here. (For a much better more in-depth discussion on this and related topics see Dr. Zakir Naik's chapter "Quran and Modern Science"). [5][6]

REASON #9

Muslims may argue that those who do not believe in God, perhaps need to think if they are willing to cry, hope, die for the entertainment of random dice rolls? (And who is rolling the dice anyway, maybe a question worth asking), After all, who wants to be a puppet in a meaningless, purposeless existence? Muslims may ask that if there is no real Justice, Truth, Compassion, Love? If there is no God, why would one want to live? For a fancy, red sports car? A summer cottage by the beach?

Muslims are very weary of any semblance of raising worldly riches or fame to the status of personal (very perishable) gods. There is a saying of Prophet Muhammad that echoes the fragility of such never-ending pursuits that are unable to quench the thirst of man, and the emptiness of his soul.

"Anas reported God's Messenger as saying: If the son of Adam were to possess two valleys of riches, he would long for the third one. And the stomach of the son of Adam is not filled but with dust. ..." (Sahih Muslim 5.2282)

Chapter End

Author's Note: Since this is a chapter on God's existence, some people may misunderstand my scientific references. I do *not* believe that God's existence (or lack thereof) can be "proved" (in an absolute sense) by science. (A Muslim might argue that this seeming ambiguity, or temporary veil, reflects a core islamic idea: freedom of choice. Freedom of choice and the slow expression of one's heart is how one's life is written out.)

God, in many ways, belongs to the realm of the "unseen" and so there is an element of faith in belief. But it is not a blind, senseless faith, God's signs are manifest throughout existence, for the thinking individual to contemplate. In fact, one is likely to find strong clues pointing to God's existence. [7]

It should also be noted that a *disbelief* in God also requires an "act of faith" in a sense (the analogy is not exact), or an axiom or assumption since the lack of existence of God cannot be scientifically proved, and there is often an implicit *assumption* that everything is humanly observable – without providing proof of that. Such individuals may say that if something is not observable it does not, for all practical purposes, exist in their world.

However as science advances and instruments become more sensitive, theories evolve and indirect experiments come online, future generations are likely to acknowledge the existence of many things and concepts that current generations would not. Modern scientists today acknowledge the existence of things the most advanced "scientist" of two thousand years ago would have categorically said did not exist or at best called fanciful speculations of highly imaginative minds. Yet just because someone from some period in time, says something does not exist does not stop it from existing, even if it is not directly observable in some fashion, through that person's eyes or senses at that time [8][9].

Chapter Endnotes:
[1] Even if extraterrestrial life was ever discovered this would not weaken the argument. Just the opposite. Such findings should raise more questions. Why are such an excessive amount of raw conditions and permutations in existence? In essence, life from *nothing* is a highly improbable event. More different life forms from nothing are even more improbable. (To digress and be a little more complete on a related point, Muslims do believe in a seperate creation (e.g. in additon to humans) called Jinn. Thtere are many definitions of the word "Jinn." One definition refers to a creation made of fire that like humans has the ability to choose between good and evil.)
[2] Another more commonly cited experiment compared two atomic (e.g. very highly accurate) clocks. One stayed stationary, the other was flown around the earth. The two times were very slightly different, and corresponded to the differences

predicted by Einstein's theory.

[3] It appears that the question of "chance" may be far more complicated than typically thought. For example, Princeton University's PEAR (Princeton Engineering Anomalies Research) lab has produced some intriguing results dealing with interaction between REGs (random event generators) and human "consciousness." Apparently, a desire or intention to "skew" chance occurrences may "shift" probablilities is a small but *statistically significant* way. (www. princeton.edu/~pear/).

[4]While parts of educated, literate Europe may have been aware of the Eratosthenes attempted Earth's circumference measurement (240 BCE) (e.g. a round earth likely based on Aristotle around 330 BCE), it is highly unlikely (although possible) that an illiterate man in Makkah (one of the most backwards societies of its time) would have been aware of such "advanced science." Long after, prophet Muhammad's death, Muslims did contribute to earth circumference measurements like during , Caliph al-Ma'mun's time (830 CE) and particularly by Abu Rayhan al-Biruni(973-1048 CE).

[5] It should be noted that even if there were "items of interest or conversation" for contemporary scientists recorded in the Quran over 1400 years ago, these point were only very recently noticed by Muslims – they were not acted on (or understood) 1400 years ago by Muslims.

[6] While European history was racked by the tumultuous relationship between science and the Church, Islam never had a similar history. Instead, Islam and science flourished hand-in-hand, as Islam strongly encouraged the pursuit of learning and knowledge. This contrasted sharply with the clashes

between science and the Church which included the famous trial of Galileo.

[7] There does seem to be tinges of some laziness and lack of humility in the approach of some agnostics that is disturbing. Two qualities that are subtly subversive, yet ultimately corrosively destructive, in the wonderfully magnificent enterprise of open exploration.

[8] There has been some interesting work done by Princeton University PEAR (Princeton Engineering Anomalies Research) studying the interaction between REGs (random event generators) and human "consciousness," as well as on "remote viewing," that suggest there may be small but statistically significant intereactions beyond our current level of understanding. There may be more dimensions of interaction than we currently understand.

[9] It would be interesting to see how some of the intriguing complexities of quantum mechanics (the physics of the small) are unraveled in the future. Today, quantum mechanics and physics suggest mind-bending concepts – that the act of observing may change the observation, that effect may precede cause (for example, empirically, there are intriguing double slit experiments on this topic) among others, that could challenge current conventional concepts of the notion of time and/or the dimensions of existence.

Islam: A Solution for America's Social Problems?

By F. Kamal

Preface: Yes, of course, one knows and acknowledges that there are many good things in American society. In many ways the US *is* a great country. But one of America's greatest strengths is that she has the courage, strength, and resilience to confront her problems and reinvent herself to address important issues. This article is written in that hope. It is also written as a witness to the numerous, faceless, tragic victims of complex, contemporary American problems. This is written in the hope that in some small way it can forestall a continued and unchecked new list of hapless victims. Note for non-American readers: Non-Americans who have not visited the US are cautioned against painting Americans with one wide, sweeping brush. Like any country, there is good and bad. In fact, there is much existing and potential good in the United States. The fact that this chapter is written by an American is a sign of the health of the US, not its dysfunction. Where "dark" spots are highlighted it is only in the hope that by shedding light on these problems, that these problems may begin to get solved.

One measure of a society is the care that it takes of its weaker, more innocent, and helpless members like the elderly and children. While there are many good things in this picture in America, there are several very disturbing blemishes. One could wonder if the symptoms reflect a spiritual vacuum and whether the antidote lies in spiritual regeneration. One may ask oneself why these blemishes are occurring. Consider the following about the elderly.

THE ELDERLY

The National Elder Abuse Incidence Study (NEAIS Final Report 1998) prepared for the U.S. Department of Health and Human Services estimates "that at least one-half million older persons in domestic settings were abused and/or neglected, or experienced self neglect during 1996, and that for every reported incident of elder abuse, neglect, or self neglect, approximately five go unreported." Within the details of the report one finds disturbing statistics like over half (51.8%) of the 80-year-plus individuals were victims of neglect in 1996, that 43.7% of the physical abuse victims were from this vulnerable age group, as were 48% of the financial/material exploitation victims. It is of grave concern when the report notes that 47.9% "of the substantiated incidents of abuse and neglect involved elderly persons who were not physically able to care for themselves." One of the most troubling parts of the report mentions that "the largest category of *perpetrators* (47.3%) of the substantiated incidents of elder abuse were the adult *children* of the victims. [1]

AN ISLAMIC PERSPECTIVE

Grandparents are integral and honored members of families in Islam. Muslims consider them indispensable and vital for the proper development of grandchildren. Islam places parents at a highly honored position. It also places strong checks on "me"-centric or materialistically driven norms and values in a society.

> Quran *17:23-24*: Thy Lord has decreed that you worship none but Him, and that you be kind to parents. Whether one or both of them attain old age in your life, say not to them a word of contempt, nor repel them, but address them in terms of honor. And, out of kindness, lower to them the wing of humility, and say: "My Lord! bestow on them Your Mercy even as they cherished me in childhood."

To financially exploit or abandon parents is simply not even an option. In Islam, parents may be *given* a share in their child's wealth if the child tries to withhold the support he is required to give them. (Sunan Abu Dawud book 23, number 3523). (Perhaps this is an acknowledgement of the unequaled and extraordinary resources of time, money, love, sacrifice, encouragement and tears that parents typically invest into their children. A child's success — and survival — typically owes much to loving parents, particularly mothers.)

A Muslim is asked by God to spend on his parents.

> *Quran 2.215;* They ask you, (O Muhammad), what they shall spend. Say: that which you spend for good (must go) to parents and near kindred

Muslims are told that there is great reward in helping parents (particularly mothers)

> Al-Tirmidhi, # 4935. Narrated Abdullah ibn Umar:

"A man came to the Prophet and said, 'Messenger of God, I have committed a serious sin. Can I do any act of penitence?' He asked him if he had a mother, and when he replied that he had not, he asked if he had a maternal aunt. On his replying that he had, he said, "Then do kindness to her.'"

One begins to understand the greatness of the rewards of caring for parents in the following hadith:

Riyadh us Saliheen, 317. Abu Hurairah reported: "The Prophet said, 'May he be disgraced! May he be disgraced! May he be disgraced, whose parents, one or both, attain old age during his life time, and he does not enter paradise (by being dutiful to the parents).'" [from Muslim].

(Note by the author: This perhaps alludes to the fact that there is such great reward in helping parents that it is hard to miss paradise if one exerts oneself well in this regard.)

CHILDREN

In 2003, 176,951 child abuse and neglect cases were substantiated in children aged 6 to 9 years, 196,150 in victims 2 to 5 years old and 127,618 in victims 1 year or younger! What did such a young child who is totally helpless do to deserve this? There were 78,188 cases of sexual abuse. [2] Another perplexing statistic is that suicide is the 6th highest cause of death in the 5 to 14 year group and the 3rd highest leading cause of death in the 15 to 24 yrs old group. [3] Why is life not a precious gift for these individuals?

Here is another disturbing statistic. Did you know that in 2003 a *juvenile* was getting arrested for a *violent* crime every 8 minutes? Clearly law enforcement is working hard, but is there a more fundamental problem in our society that police officers cannot really address? The breakdown of the juvenile arrest numbers is 45,955 for aggravated assault, 18,950 for robbery, 3,195 for forcible rape, and 960 for murder. [4]

There are also some very tragic numbers about young victims of murder – some very young. In 2003, there were 312 murders where the victim was 1 to 4 years old and 231 murders of infants under 1 year. [5] Surely such a tragedy deserves some reflection and action.

SEXUAL PROMISCUITY IS RAMPANT IN THE USA AND IT IS HARMING HER CHILDREN

The majority of American adolescents had engaged in sexual intercourse by age 17 in 1997 (62% in-school females; 60% in-school males). Of course, this has consequences. In fact, more than 12 million acquire STDs (Sexually Transmitted Diseases) every year with adolescents and young adults at particularly high risk. This makes it the most commonly reported disease in the United States. Some of the health consequences of STDs can include infertility, congenital defects, blindness, cancer, and death. [6]

Also despite many common beliefs about contraception, the failure rate on contraception is quite high. 13.8% of women experienced contraceptive failure during the first 12 months of use. Certain population sub-groups experienced alarmingly high failure rates. For example, 51.3% of women experienced contraceptive failure during the first 12 months of use in the "ever married, < 200% of poverty, with condom use" sub-group. [7]

Sex (outside marriage) and contraception failure have consequences. Let us examine abortions. In 2002, there were 1,293,000 abortions in the United States. This means that in four months a population roughly the size of nation of Luxemburg was wiped out, in a year a population roughly the size of the country of Estonia would be wiped out, or equivalently in about 3 years the entire population of the nation of Ireland. This would mean that over an average American's lifespan (e.g. 77 years) around twenty five Irelands would have disappeared. (And we are looking at only US, not world, abortions.)

Now for some interesting facts about the abortions. Did you know that the ratio of abortions to live births in 2002 was 319 per 1,000 live births? Does that not seem to be an alarmingly high rate? Did you know that abortions were not a one time thing for an unusually high percent of individuals? Instead of learning from the past, in 2001, 46% had already had one or more prior induced abortions. Was abortion being used like birth control? But perhaps the most revealing statistic about abortions is the number concerning the martial status of the woman. 82% were unmarried. [8]

FAMILY

This last statistic gives us an important inkling or clue of what might be going wrong. The American family is losing fundamental ground. Unfortunately, the American family though very resilient, is under severe attack. Here are the facts, and what better indicator of the well-being of children than to look at the state of the nation's households.

After all, the family – and parents in particular – can provide a strong protective and nurturing environment for children, a safe haven in bad weather and a source of joy and strength in other times. While many individual parents have discharged their duties heroically, unfortunately the institution of family itself has come under considerable stress and in many cases seems to be seriously weakened.

The state of U.S. families for children ages 15 to 17 in 1996. Here is the breakdown nationally: Married couple (biological/adoptive/stepparent) 65.9%; single parent (mom/dad) 24.8%; no parent 6.0%; cohabiting/partner 3.4%. [9] Common sense suggests that two good married parents raising children have less stress and access to considerably more resources than just one—just like running with one's own two good legs is much easier than hopping on one. It appears that the family's ability to shield and cushion its children from shocks has certainly diminished over the years – as it has suffered from its own problems.

MOTHERS AND FATHERS

Since families are so critical to the health of society as a whole, it deserves a closer look. Here are some possible factors affecting the breakdown of families:

The plight of the concept of motherhood in America today. While there are many good individual mothers in America today, the messages American society as a whole is sending mothers is much more mixed. In fact, today in America few things seem to be given as little weight as motherhood. It is unusual in the history of mankind that so little apparent emphasis or value is given to so fundamental and extraordinarily essential a pillar of society. Such a nonchalant disregard for motherhood surely bodes ill for the United States. Slowly, but surely, the concepts of sacrifice, dedication, perspective, and perseverance seem to be being eroded from the institutional nomenclature of American motherhood. Instead it appears we face the embarrassment of having coined the terms "quality time" and "latchkey children" in this U.S. generation.

Mothers in Islam, enjoy a position of extraordinary honor and respect. In many ways, Muslim mothers are the linchpin of families, and families are at the core of Muslim communities. Muslims believe, the value of good Muslim women cannot be underestimated. There are many, many explicit statements in the Quran and Sunnah concretely establishing the unique and treasured position of these good women. Muslims are reminded of their duties to their mothers and are enjoined to treat them in the most excellent of manners.

And we have enjoined men to treat their parents well (in the first instance, the mother). His mother bore him with such difficulty and suffered so much in giving him birth. (Quran 46:15)

O mankind! Be careful of your duty to your Lord Who created you from a single soul and from it its mate and from them both have spread abroad a multitude of men and women. Be careful of your duty toward God in Whom you claim (your rights) of one another, and towards the wombs (that bore you). Lo! God has been a Watcher over you. (Quran 4:1)

And here is a hadith concerning the honor of a good Muslim mother to be accorded by her son.

Riyadh us Saliheen, 316: Abu Huraira reported: "A person came to the Messenger of God and asked, 'Who among people is most deserving of my fine treatment?" He said, 'Your mother.' He again asked, `'Who next? Your mother,' the Prophet replied again. He asked, 'Who next?" He (the Prophet) said again, Your mother." He again asked, 'Then who?' Thereupon he said, 'Then your father.' In another narration: 'O Messenger of God! Who is most deserving of my fine treatment?' He said, 'Your mother, then your mother, then your mother, then your father, then your nearest, then nearest.'" (Al-Bukhari and Muslim).

It is hard to imagine a religious statement that could raise a good woman to a higher level of honor. After all, what could that religious statement be? These and many other statements also show how ludicrously inaccurate are any allegations that Islam is "anti-woman." (Note: While some Muslims may act in ways that unfairly hurt women, these actions are clearly *unislamic*.)

Islam clearly establishes a great reward for a good mother. There are few rewards as great for a pious Muslim than to be assured of the Prophet's close company during the Day of Resurrection.

Sunan Abu Dawud, book 41, number 5130: Narrated Awf ibn Malik al-Ashja'i': "The Prophet said: 'I and a woman whose cheeks have become black shall on the Day of Resurrection be like these two (pointing to the middle and forefinger), i.e,. a woman of rank and beauty who has been bereft of her husband and devotes herself to her fatherless children until they go their separate ways or die. '"

Riyadh us Saliheen, 269: `Aishah reported: "A poor woman came to me carrying her two daughters. I gave her three dates. She gave a date to each of them and then she took up one date and brought that to her mouth to eat, but her daughters asked her for that also. She then divided between them the date that she intended to eat. This (kind) treatment of her impressed me and I mentioned that to the Messenger of God who said, 'Verily, God has assured paradise for her, because of (this act) of her," or said, "He has rescued her from the fires of Hell.'" [Muslim].

The abandonment by men of their responsibilities for being husbands is seriously damaging families. While the demise of motherhood as an integral and valued component of society has been much more visible, the collapse of the role men play in families, although more subtle, has been no less severe.

In Islam, men are enjoined to maintain and protect their families (*Surah an-Nisa, Quran*). In fact, many non-Muslims may be surprised to discover that Muslim husbands normally have NO right to their wives' wealth. Therefore, even if one's wife is independently and fabulously wealthy, she could conceivably demand a right to be financially maintained without the husband touching any of her money! (However, on a practical or emotional level it may not be the smartest move on the part of a spouse to withold money from a spouse in financial trouble.) If the husband is experiencing financial difficulties, many Muslim women have instead chosen to *voluntarily* help their husbands out of a love for God and their families.

Men are so strongly exhorted not to be lazy or selfish in providing for a family, that if a man does not give his wife money, she has a right to take (a small, reasonable) amount under certain circumstances. (*Sunan Abu Dawud #3525*). Ultimately, many practicing Muslim men provide for their families because it normally brings out the best in them, and because they seek to please their Lord. (Laziness is discouraged in both men and women.) Muslim men and women believe anything that brings out the best in themselves will ultimately be rewarded by God. [10]

The importance of parenting and raising good children. Muslims are strongly exhorted to care for their children:

Sunan Abu Dawud book 41, number 5128: Narrated AbuSa'id al-Khudri: "The Prophet said: 'If anyone cares for three daughters, disciplines them, finds them husbands, and does good to them, he will go to Paradise.'"

Marriage has lost some luster, as evidenced by the statistics on cohabiting/partner couples with families. In sharp contrast, marriage is very highly valued in Islamic societies, and there is much reward attached to it.

When man has married, he has completed one half of his religion. Then let him fear God for the remaining half. *(Baihaqi)*

What a ringing endorsement of marriage, Muslims note!

Islam provides and values such a diverse and interlocking set of instructions to protect the Muslim family from breakup, because the consequences for society of family breakdowns are real and severe. For example, statistically one of the strongest predictors of crime is belonging to a single-parent home. The Department of Justice publication "Profile of Jail Inmates, 1996" (http://www.ojp.usdoj.gov/bjs/pub/ascii/pji96.txt) states, " Relative to the general population, jail inmates were over twice as likely to have grown up in a single-parent household."

SOME CRIME STATISTICS

In 2003, every 23 seconds there was a violent crime

in America. A murder was reported every 31 minutes. There was a forcible rape once every 6 minutes, one robbery every minute and an aggravated assault every 37 seconds. [11] These are sobering statistics for anyone interested in the welfare of this nation. Unfortunately the real numbers are much higher since the actual incidence of violence is higher than the reported cases. So rape/sexual assault were actually estimated to take place every 3 minutes each day. Actual aggravated assault was closer to once every 29 seconds each day, and robbery once every 53 seconds. [12]

Sometimes it has been said that crime is caused by poverty. While it is true that sometimes wealth can be used to fight crime, the relationship between poverty and crime is far more complex and not always conclusive. There have also been poor Muslim communities in history that were vibrant with Islam that appear to have had low crime rates.

Today the United States, perhaps the richest nation in human history, actually holds the world's highest incarceration rate at 714 per 100,000 of population. [13] There were a record 5.9 million U.S. adults behind bars or under police supervision in 1999. [14] Is the true root of the problem really more complex? Is there perhaps a spiritual emptiness that is spawning a resulting moral crisis in our nation?

SLAVERY

It may appear shocking that slavery exists today in many ugly degrading forms. What may be even more disconcerting is that it exists here, today, in the United

States! Driven by an unchecked sexual explosion, fanned by several irresponsible elements of the mass media, several sick, disturbed cesspools of sexuality have left a grotesque mark on our societies.

Lured by false promises of American riches and outright lies, some women from Eastern Europe, the Far East, and Mexico have come to our shores only to find that they have, in reality, been forced into notorious American sex rings. There they are forced to perform degrading acts against their will -- held hostage under the heartless grip of the modern face of slavery. Beatings, intimidation, and brutal "disciplinary" rapes by their captors force them to toe the line. [15] It is a veritable prison, a modern-day, American (sex) slave camp for them .

Not only has the cruel sexual lust of a small segment of American society destroyed the lives of countless women, even equally tragic, if not more so, are the gut-wrenching stories of child sex rings. Today, reflecting the reality of our society, an American parent must warn young children—as young as six – about not speaking to strangers, entering cars with strangers, etc. A mother must contend with the thought that her precious child could be kidnapped and have unspeakable acts committed on him/her by a twisted pedophile. [16] In fact, the heinous nature of crimes today should be a clear wake up call about a crisis in American society. For deep-thinking Americans willing to scratch below the surface, it should be of profound concern when he or she hears about yet another serial killer, pedophile, or rape on TV. What causes a serial killer to commit his demented acts of hacking up a body to pieces and much worse?

In an interview Ted Bundy (an infamous American serial killer) significantly selected to highlight the impact he perceived pornography had on his development and the influence he felt it had on his fellow inmates in prison. To better understand killers we can also refer to the FBI's National Center for the Analysis of Violent Crime. The FBI highlights three factors that figure prominently in the background of a killer. An inability to establish an emotional bond with one's mother, lack of parental role models, and being a victim of physical or sexual abuse are important components of the FBI profile of a killer. [17]

MODESTY & PROMISCUITY

Then why this explosion of promiscuity in American society?

Today, mass media is saturated with sexual themes, suggestive content, and innuendoes. In fact, it takes considerable effort today to avoid the deluge of billboards, ads, and gratuitous music using sex to sell a product. Even cartoons directed at children today have some sexual overtones! The very fabric that American society rests on today has been transformed dramatically from what existed only a few decades ago – and as America's values have been compromised, so too have her norms changed. In 1995, in the United States, 66% of women, aged 15-44, reported having more than one male sexual partner in their lifetime. Here is the lifetime breakdown in terms of number of partners by percentage. 0: 10.5%; 1: 23.5%; 2: 12.3%; 3: 9.6%; 4: 8.4%; 5: 8.1%;

6-9: 12.1%; and 10 or more partners: 15.5%. [18] In 2002, 34% births occurred to unmarried mothers. [19]

In Islam, modesty is an extremely important part of the faith. Hijab (head covering), a symbol of Muslim women, is an example of modesty as a part of faith -- modesty as a means of seeking the pleasure of God.

> *Sahih Bukhari volume 1, book 2, number 8:* Narrated Abu Huraira: "The Prophet said, 'Faith (belief) consists of more than sixty branches (i.e. parts). And Haya (this term, Haya, covers a large number of concepts that are to be taken together, among which are self respect, modesty, bashfulness, and scruple.) is a part of faith.'"

Islam has many safeguards against a breakdown of society's sexual norms. For example, one of the contemporary problems of American society seems to be the de-facto (as opposed to theoretical) abdication of some parents taking parental responsibility for the virginity of their children. How many parents nowadays actively and vigorously work to protect the pre-marital sexuality of their children? And for how many is it almost a casual afterthought – something to be done time permitting? Or how about: "pre-marital sex is not all that bad – everyone does it?" While it should be noted that many parents do care, perhaps not enough, care enough.

Yet from a Muslim perspective, as an example, a Muslim father is informed that he bears responsibility for protecting the chastity of his son (source: Baihaqi) before marriage. A son's failure, or sin, in this regard may also lie with a (negligent and irresponsible) father. The onset of puberty signals the beginning of the time the parent must begin to show real vigilance for their children. Of course, one is **not** responsible if one discharges one's duties truly to the best of one's abilities and things do not turn out right. ("No laden soul will bear another's load," Quran 39:7, and see the case of Noah's son in Quran 11:45-46).

INTOXICANTS

While broken families and pornography play critical roles in crimes, so too do intoxicants. In fact let us examine the extraordinary correlation between alcohol/drugs and crime.

Did you know the following for example? 51.9 % of state prisoners had alcohol or drug use at the time they committed violent crimes! The numbers are 52.4% for murder, 56.0% for negligent manslaughter, 45.2% for sexual assault, 55.5% for robbery, and 51.8% for assault. [20]

Many gruesome war crimes and atrocities have also long been committed by the plundering armies' officers and enlisted men high on alcohol. The strong link between intoxicants and destructive violence is not a surprise to Muslims. The Quran says the following about intoxicants. (In Quran 5.90 Intoxicants are prohibited.)

> Quran, *5:90* O you who believe! Intoxicants and gambling, (dedication of) stones, and (divination by) arrows are an abomination of Satan's handwork: avoid such (abomination), so you may prosper.

The next ayah (verse) is interesting since it hints at some possible problems with intoxicants.

> Quran 5:91: Satan's plan is (only) to excite enmity and hatred among you with intoxicants and gambling, and to hinder you from the remembrance of God and from prayer; will you not then abstain?

Islamic communities are one of the very few societies in human history that have had large scale, verifiable success against intoxicants over very long periods of time – avoiding countless problems.

CONCLUSION

The preceding accounts have explored some of America's social problems and suggested how Islam could potentially be an effective and powerful counter weight to so many of these interlocked, contemporary problems.

Some Questions

Question: Can not individuals from other faith traditions, or otherwise, also make a society better?

Response: Of course they can. Many societies have special people, hard working and dedicated, that help contribute towards improving and beautifying a society.

Question: Do not some Muslim majority nations suffer from problems like corruption and human rights abuse?

Response:

Of course not all Muslims behave Islamically. So , for example, while Islam may have strong injunctions against intoxicants, a small minority of Muslims may choose to behave unislamically and ignore those injunctions and some people may suffer some of the profound problems associated with the abuse of alcohol and/or illegal drugs. This principle could be applied to other cases where a few Muslims choose to violate or ignore basic Islamic teachings.

On a wider note, it should be noted that things like parasitic corruption, abuse of power, and degrading torture have sometimes been found in Muslim majority locations. Unfortunately, some "Muslims" can, and do commit unislamic acts.   This book is about Islam, not about Muslims who engage in acts that directly *contradict* their religion. Muslims would argue that if these individuals were diligently following Islam such acts would not be occurring. In such cases, they would say that it is not Islam, but in fact the opposite —the lack of Islam — that was an important source of some of these distressing problems.

Corruption

"And do not eat up your property among yourselves for vanities, nor use it as bait for the judges, with intent that you may eat up wrongfully and knowingly a little of (other) people's property." Quran 2.188

Torture/Oppression

The prophet also stated that God said: "I have forbidden oppression ... so do not oppress one another" Hadith Qudsi 17.

Another area Muslim majority countires can do a better job in is the pursuit of knowledge. Despite a very strong emphasis in the sayings of prophet Muhammad on seeking knowledge, a significant cross section of comtemporary Muslims can do a much better job in living up to what Islam expects of them in this sphere.

"Seeking knowledge is obligatory upon every Muslim." Sunan Ibn Majah. (220)

"...the best are the virtuous among the learned" Mishkat ul Masabih #267

"If anyone travels on a road in search of knowledge, God will cause him to travel on one of the roads of Paradise. The angels will lower their wings in their great pleasure with one who seeks knowledge... Sunan Abu Dawud, Book 25, Number 3634:

"...and say: My Lord! Increase me in knowledge" Quran 20:114

SOURCES

U.S. Census Bureau, Statistical Abstract of the United States (SAUS). http://www.census.gov/statab/www/ 2006 & 1999 and others as noted.

[1]www.aoa.gov/eldfam/Elder_Rights/Elder_Abuse/ABuseReport_Full.pdf
[2] 2006 SAUS #332
[3] 2006 SAUS #109
[4] 2006 SAUS #316
[5] 2006 SAUS #298
[6] Source: National Center for Health Statistics. Healthy People 2000 Review, 1998-99. Hyattsville, Maryland: Public Health Service. 1999.
[7] Family Planning Perspectives, Volume 24, Number 1, January/February 1992, "Contraceptive Failure Rates Based on the 1988 NSFG," Elise F. Jones and Jacqueline Darroch Forrest (From Tables 2 & 3)
[8] 2006 SAUS #93 & #94
[9] http://www.childstats.gov/ac2000/pop5B.htm (source: U.S. Census Bureau, Survey of Income and Program Participation.)
[10]Of course, this does not exclude women from working outside the home (particularly if there are no small children or elderly parents.) For example, few men are excited by lazy wives who only fritter away their days away in idle gossip and frivolous shopping.
[11] 2006 SAUS #293.
[12]2006 SAUS #309.
[13] Roy Walmsley, World Prison Population List. (Sixth edition).
[14]http://www.cnn.com August 22, 1999 "Number of U.S. offenders reaches record 5.9 million." Source:

Bureau of Justice Statistics.

[15] CNN.com (Reuters) August 31, 2000 "U.S. grapples with 'modern-day slavery'" is one such news report.

[16] For more information: http://www.missingkids.org/html/publications_ list.html. (The national Center for missing and exploited children website.)

[17] Criminal Investigative Analysis: Sexual Homicide, 1990, FBI, National Center for the Analysis of Violent Crime.

[18] 1999 SAUS #110

[19] 2006 SAUS #80

[20] 1999 SAUS #383

God and Muslims

By F. Kamal

I remember reading about an American Muslim's journey of discovery. She had, I recall, noted that Eskimos had 200 names for the word "snow." Obviously it played an important role in the lives of Eskimos. It was also noted that Americans had many terms for the word money. (Buck, greenback, grand, dough, moola are some that come to mind). Money certainly plays an important role in popular American culture. It then struck her how Muslims had 99 names for God. Here are a few of those names for God.

Ar-Rahmaan
  The Compassionate, The Beneficent

Ar-Raheem
  The Merciful

Did you know that *every* Chapter (except one) in the Quran begins in the name of Ar-Rahmaan, Ar-Raheem. This gives great comfort to Muslims.

Al-Wadood
  The Loving

And He [God] is the Forgiving, the Loving" Quran 85.14-16

... And God is always close to you. "We verily created man and We know what his soul whispers to him, and We are nearer to him than his jugular vein." Quran 50:16 As Muslims would note, it is not possible for Him to be closer to you, so one should never despair of God's sublime presence.

Al-Ghaffaar
The Great Forgiver, The Forgiver

Al-Adl
The Just

Al-Kareem
The Generous One, The Bountiful, The Gracious

Did you know that Muslim "accounting" is unique among religions?

Sahih Bukhari 8.498: The Prophet narrated about his Lord, "God ordered (the appointed angels over you) that the good and the bad deeds be written, and He then showed (the way) how (to write). If somebody intends to do a good deed and he does not do it, then God will write for him a full good deed (in his account with Him); and if he intends to do a good deed and actually did it, then God will write for him (in his account) with Him (its reward equal) from ten to seven hundred times to many more times: and if somebody intended to do a bad deed and he does not do it, then God will write a full good deed (in his account) with Him, and if he intended to do it (a bad deed) and actually did it, then God will write one bad deed (in his account)."

God is indeed very generous to Muslims.

Al-Hakeem
The Wise, The Judge of Judges

Al-Aleem
The All-knowing, The Knowledgeable

Al-Mujeeb
The Responsive, The Hearkener

As-Salaam
The Source of Peace

Thus it is obvious that it is an extraordinary *privilege* for Muslims to strive to place God at the center of their lives. But worshiping God and placing Him at the center of one's life is not to benefit God but rather the individual. It should be obvious by now that man's submission to God is not for God's benefit but for ours.

Consider this saying:
Abu Dharr reported God's Messenger as saying that God said: My servants, I have made oppression unlawful for Me and unlawful for you, so do not

commit oppression against one another. My servants, all of you are liable to err except one whom I guide on the right path, so seek right guidance from Me so that I should direct you to the right path. O My servants, all of you are hungry except one whom I feed, so ask food from Me, so that I may give that to you. O My servants, all of you are naked except one whom I provide garments, so ask clothes from Me, so that I should clothe you. O My servants, you commit error night and day and I am there to pardon your sins, so ask pardon from Me so that I can grant you pardon. O My servants, you can neither do Me any harm nor can you do Me any good. O My servants, even if the whole human race, and that of jinns, became as pious as the most of pious of you nothing would add to My Power. O My servants, even the whole human race and that of the Jinns became like the most wicked of you, it would cause no loss to My Power. O My servants, even if the first amongst you and the last amongst you and the whole human race and that of jinns also were to all stand up and ask of Me and I confer upon every person what he asks for, it would not. in any way, cause any loss to Me (even less) than that which is caused to the ocean by dipping the needle in it. My servants, your deeds will be accrued and I shall compensate you for them, so if you find any good in your deeds, praise God, and as for him who finds otherwise in his deeds, do not blame anyone but your ownself.
(Sahih Muslim Book 032, Number 6246)

But if you count the favors of God, never will you be able to number them. Quran 14:34

Some Muslim Virtues (Quran)

By A.W.

There is no better way to learn about Islam than to read the Holy Qur'an and to observe the practices of a devout Muslim. Unfortunately, the many stereotypes, misconceptions, and misrepresentations prevalent today serve as a great barrier that prevents non-Muslims from understanding the truth about Islam. Lack of access to an English translation of the Qur'an and, moreover, to a knowledgeable Muslim who represents Islam well may also be factors. Therefore, it is a hope that this [chapter] will assist those who desire to know exactly what the Qur'an teaches and how a practicing Muslim is supposed to act.

The Holy Qur'an, the revelation given to Prophet Muhammad almost 1400 years ago, is an instruction book for people of all times and all places on how one can live one's life correctly. It contains therein, among other things, the qualities that one should adopt in order to please the Creator and to obtain true peace on Earth. The ultimate result from a sincere striving toward such qualities would be the fulfillment of the human being's purpose in this life (submission to the One God) and the attainment of the reward in the next life (eternal Paradise!)

This brief work is meant to convey the moral standard

by which the conscious Muslim lives his or her life according to Islam. These moral teachings have been extrapolated from the Holy Qur'an, a book which Muslims believe is the final revelation of the Creator to His creation. Muslims use this book as a standard for correct faith and action because they have a firm belief that the Creator knows what is best for His creation. In the Holy Qur'an, God says, "Verily this Qur'an guides to what is most right" (17:9). Muslims believe that submission to the One God and commitment to the teachings of divine scripture are essential means to solving the problems of the world.

RIGHTEOUSNESS

"Do no evil nor mischief on the (face of the) earth" (2:60).

"Let there arise out of you a band of people inviting to all that is good, enjoining what is right, and forbidding what is wrong" (3:104).

"Do good to parents, kinsfolk, orphans, those in need, neighbors who are of kin, neighbors who are strangers, the companion by your side, the wayfarer (you meet), and what your right hands possess" (4:36).

"[God] forbids all indecent deeds and evil and rebellion: He instructs you, that you may receive admonition" (16:90).

"Verily the most honored of you in the sight of God is (he who is) the most righteous of you" (49:13).

GENEROSITY

"Give of the good things which you have (honorably) earned, and of the fruits of the earth which We have produced for you" (2:267).

"If you disclose (acts of) charity, even so it is well, but if you conceal them and make them reach those (really) in need, that is best for you" (2:271).

"By no means shall you attain righteousness unless you give (freely) of that which you love." (3:92)

"Those saved from the covetousness of their own souls, are the ones who achieve prosperity" (59:9).

"[Do not] expect, in giving, any increase (for yourself)!" (74:6).

GRATITUDE

"Eat of the good things that We have provided for you, and be grateful to God, if it is Him you worship" (2:172).

"Show gratitude to Me and to your parents: to Me is (your final) Goal" (31:14).

"[God] does not like ingratitude from His servants; if you are grateful, He is pleased with you" (39:7).

CONTENTMENT

"In no wise covet those things in which God has bestowed His gifts more freely on some of you than on others: to men is allotted what they earn, and to women what they earn: but ask God of His bounty" (4:32).

HUMILITY

"Call on your Lord with humility and in private: for God does not love those who trespass beyond bounds" (7:55).

"Celebrate the praises of your Lord, and be of those who prostrate themselves in adoration" (15:98).

"The servants of (God) Most Gracious are those who walk on the earth in humility, and, when the ignorant address them, say, 'Peace!'" (25:63).

"Do not exult, for God does not love those who exult (in riches)" (28:76).

"Swell not your cheek (for pride) at men, nor walk in insolence through the earth; for God does not love any arrogant boaster" (31:18).

KINDNESS

"God loves those who are kind." (5:13)

"Be kind to parents. Whether one or both of them attain old age in your life, do not say to them a word of contempt, nor repel them, but address them in terms of honor. And, out of kindness, lower to them the wing of humility, and say: 'My Lord! bestow on them Your Mercy even as they cherished me in childhood'" (17:23-24).

"We have enjoined on man (to be good) to his parents: in travail upon travail did his mother bear him, and in years twain was his weaning" (31:14).

"Do not treat the orphan with harshness, nor repulse him who asks" (93:9-10).

COURTESY

"When a (courteous) greeting is offered you, meet it with a greeting still more courteous, or (at least) of equal courtesy. God takes careful account of all things" (4:86).

"Let not some men among you laugh at others: it may be that the (latter) are better than the (former): nor let some women laugh at others: it may be that the (latter) are better than the (former): nor defame nor be sarcastic to each other, nor call each other by (offensive) nicknames" (49:11).

PURITY

"Eat of what is on the earth, lawful and good; and do not follow the footsteps of Satan, for he is to you an avowed enemy" (2:168).

"[God] loves those who keep themselves pure and clean" (2:222).

"When you prepare for prayer, wash your faces, and your hands (and arms) to the elbows; rub your heads (with water); and (wash) your feet to the ankles. If you are in a state of ceremonial impurity, bathe your whole body... God doth not wish to place you in difficulty, but to make you clean" (5:6).

GOOD SPEECH

"Say to My servants that they should say (only) those things that are best: for Satan sows dissensions among them" (17:53).

"[The believers] have been guided ... to the purest of speeches" (22:24).

"Woe to every (kind of) scandal-monger and backbiter" (104:1).

RESPECT

"Say to the People of the Book and to those who are unlearned: 'Do you (also) submit yourselves?' If they do, they are in right guidance, but if they turn back, your duty is to convey the Message" (3:20).

"Enter not houses other than your own, until you have asked permission and greeted those in them: this is best for you, in order that you may heed (what is seemly). If you find no one in the house, do not enter until permission is given to you: if you are asked to go back, go back: that makes for greater purity for yourselves" (24:27-28).

"Avoid suspicion as much (as possible), for suspicion in some cases is a sin and do not spy on each other nor speak ill of each other behind their backs. Would any of you like to eat the flesh of his dead brother?" (49:12).

WISDOM

"Invite (all) to the Way of Your Lord with wisdom and beautiful preaching; and argue with them in ways that are best and most gracious" (16:125).

TOLERANCE

"Say: 'O People of the Book! come to common terms as between us and you: That we worship none but God; that we associate no partners with Him; that we erect not, from among ourselves, lords and patrons other than God.' If then they turn back, say: 'Bear witness that we (at least) are Muslims (bowing to God's Will)" (3:64).

"If it had been your Lord's Will, they would all have believed, all who are on earth! Would you then compel people, against their will, to believe!" (10:99)

JUSTICE

"Stand out firmly for justice, as witnesses to God, even as against yourselves, or your parents, or your kin, and whether it be (against) rich or poor: for God can best protect both. Follow not the lusts (of your hearts), lest you swerve" (4:135).

"God loves those who judge in equity." (5:42)

"Do not take life, which God hath made sacred, except by way of justice and law" (6:151).

MERCY
"If the debtor is in a difficulty, grant him time until it is easy for him to repay. But if you remit it by way of charity, that is best for you if you only knew" (2:280).

"We ordained therein for them: 'Life for life, eye for an eye, nose for a nose, ear for an ear, tooth for a tooth, and wounds equal for equal.' But if any one remits the retaliation by way of charity, it is an act of atonement for himself" (5:45).

"Overlook (any human faults) with gracious forgiveness" (15:85).

"Repel (Evil) with what is better: then will the person between whom and you was hatred become as it were your friend and intimate!" (41:34).

"Those who believe and put their trust in their Lord ... forgive even when they are angry" (42:36-37).

"The recompense for an injury is an injury equal thereto (in degree), but if a person forgives and makes reconciliation, his reward is due from God, for (God) does not love those who do wrong" (42:40).

DIGNITY

"To those against whom war is made, permission is

given (to fight), because they are wronged" (22:39).

"If any do help and defend themselves after a wrong (done) to them, against such there is no cause of blame" (42:41).

COURAGE

"Those who believe ... when an oppressive wrong is inflicted on them, (are not cowed but) help each other and defend themselves" (42:36-39).

FIRMNESS

"How many of the Prophets fought (in God's way), and with them (fought) large bands of godly men? But they never lost heart if they met with disaster in God's way, nor did they weaken (in will) nor give in. And God loves those who are firm and steadfast" (3:146).

"Bear with patient constancy whatever happens to you for this is firmness (of purpose) in (the conduct of) affairs" (31:17).

FRANKNESS

"Fear God, and make your utterance straight forward, so He may make your conduct whole and sound" (33:70-71).

HOPE

"Here is a plain statement to men, a guidance and instruction to those who fear God. So lose not heart, nor fall into despair: For you must gain mastery if you are true in Faith" (3:138-139).

"What is with you must vanish: what is with God will endure. And We will certainly bestow on those who patiently persevere their reward according to the best of their actions" (16:96).

PATIENCE

"Seek (God's) help with patient perseverance and prayer. It is indeed hard, except to those who are humble, who bear in mind the certainty that they are to meet their Lord and that they are to return to Him" (2:45-46).

"Be sure we shall test you with something of fear and hunger, some loss in goods or lives or the fruits (of your toil), but give glad tidings to those who patiently persevere, who say, when afflicted with calamity 'To God We belong, and to Him is our return'. These are the ones on whom blessings (descend) from their Lord and Mercy" (2:155-157).

"Pray for help from God, and (wait) in patience and constancy: for the earth is God's to give as a heritage to such of His servants as He pleases; and the end is (best) for the righteous" (7:128).

PERSEVERANCE

"On no soul does God place a burden greater than it can bear. It gets every good that it earns, and it suffers every ill that it earns" (2:286).

"You shall certainly be tried and tested in your possessions and in your personal selves; and you shall certainly hear much that will grieve you from those who received the Book before you and from those who worship partners besides God. But, if you persevere patiently and guard against evil, then that will be of great resolution" (3:186).

DISCIPLINE

"Bow down, prostrate yourselves, and adore your Lord; and do good so that you may prosper. And strive in His cause as you ought to strive (with sincerity and under discipline)" (22:77-78).

SELF-RESTRAINT

"Fasting is prescribed for you as it was prescribed for those before you, so that you may (learn) self-restraint" (2:183).

"[Do not follow] the lust (of your heart), for it will mislead you from the Path of God" (38:26).

"For such as had entertained the fear of standing before their Lord's (tribunal) and had restrained (their) soul from lower desires, their abode will be the Garden" (79:40-41).

BALANCE / MODERATION

"Fight in the cause of God those who fight you, but do not transgress limits; for God does not love transgressors" (2:190).

"Commit no excess: for God does not love those given to excess" (5:87).

"And the servants of (God) Most Gracious are those who ... when they spend, are not extravagant and not niggardly, but hold a just (balance) between those (extremes)" (25:63-67).

"Seek, with the (wealth) that God has bestowed on you, the Home of the Hereafter, and do not forget your portion in this world: but do good, as God has been good to you." (28:77)

PRUDENCE

"When you deal with each other, in transactions involving future obligations in a fixed period of time, reduce them to writing ... whether it be small or big; it is more just in the sight of God, more suitable as evidence, and more convenient to prevent doubts among yourselves" (2:282).

"If a wicked person comes to you with any news, ascertain the truth, lest you harm people unwittingly, and afterwards become full of repentance for what you have done" (49:6).

UNITY

"Hold fast, all together, by the Rope that God (stretches out for you), and do not be divided among yourselves; and remember with gratitude God's favor on you; for you were enemies and He joined your hearts in love so that by His Grace, you became brothers" (3:103).

FRUGALITY

"Do not eat up your property among yourselves in vanities" (4:29).

"Do not waste by excess: for God does not love the wasters" (6:141).

SINCERITY

"God will never change the grace that He has bestowed on a people until they change what is in their (own) souls" (8:53).

"Woe to the worshippers ... who (want only) to be seen" (107:4-6).

RESPONSIBILITY

"Whoever recommends and helps a good cause becomes a partner therein; and whoever recommends and helps an evil cause shares in its burden" (4:85).

LOYALTY

"Fulfill (every) engagement, for (every) engagement will be inquired into (on the Day of Reckoning)" (17:34).

TRUSTWORTHINESS

"If one of you deposits a thing on trust with another, let the trustee (faithfully) discharge his trust, and let him fear God" (2:283).

"God commands you to render back your trusts to those to whom they are due" (4:58).

HONESTY / FAIR-DEALING

"Do not cover Truth with falsehood, nor conceal the Truth when you know (what it is)" (2:42).

"Do not take your oaths, to practice deception between yourselves." (16:94)

"Truly many are the partners (in business) who wrong each other. Not so do those who believe and work deeds of righteousness, and how few are they?" (38:24).

"Woe to those that deal in fraud, those who, when they have to receive by measure from men, exact full measure, but when they have to give by measure or weight to men, give less than what is due" (83:1-3).

REPENTANCE

"Seek you the forgiveness of your Lord, and turn to Him in repentance so that He may grant you enjoyment good (and true) for a term appointed" (11:3).

"Your Lord knows best what is in your hearts. If you do deeds of righteousness, verily He is Most Forgiving to those who turn to Him again and again (in true penitence)" (17:25).

SPIRITUALITY

"Behold! In the creation of the heavens and the earth, and the alternation of night and day, there are indeed Signs for men of understanding, men who celebrate the praises of God, standing, sitting, and lying down on their sides, and contemplate the (wonders of) creation in the heavens and the earth, (with the thought): 'Our Lord! not for naught have You created (all) this! Glory to Thee!'" (3:190-191)

"Establish regular prayer, for prayer restrains from shameful and evil deeds; and remembrance of God is the greatest (thing in life) without doubt" (29:45).

"True, there is for you by day prolonged occupation with ordinary duties, but keep in remembrance the name of Your Lord and devote yourself to Him whole-heartedly. (He is) Lord of the East and the West there is no god but He, take Him therefore for your Disposer of Affairs" (73:7-9).

10

Some Muslim Virtues (Sayings of the Prophet)

By A.W.

The Holy Qur'an is the highest authority in Islam. Muslims believe, it contains the exact words of God as revealed to Prophet Muhammad and recorded by his companions. In applying the Qur'anic teachings to everyday life, Muslims rely upon the sunnah (sayings and actions) of the Prophet . According to Muslim tradition, this sunnah is a concrete implementation, a tangible form, and an embodiment of the will of God in the form of Muhammad's deeds. They were recorded in what are called ahadith (pieces of news, stories, or reports). This [chapter] conveys to you just a portion of the many interesting and enlightening ahadith. Numbers 1-19 have been extrapolated from "Riyadh-Us-Saleheen" Volumes 1 and 2. Numbers 20-24 have been extrapolated from "An-Nawawi's Forty Hadith." Both works were compiled by Imam Abu Zakariya Yahya Bin Sharaf An-Nawawi. Each hadith quoted in this pamphlet is followed by an individual reference that indicates the original source of ahadith collection: Imam Bukhari, Imam Muslim, Imam Abu Daud, or Imam Tirmidhi.

1) Abu Hurairah relates that the Holy Prophet said: "The strong man is not one who is good at wrestling, but the strong man is one who controls himself in a fit of rage" (Bukhari and Muslim). RAS Vol 1, #45.

2) Abu Hurairah relates that the Holy Prophet said: "It does not befit a Siddiq (righteous Muslim) to frequently curse others." (Muslim). RAS Vol 2, #1552

3) Jarir Ibn Abdullah relates that the Holy Prophet said: "He who is not merciful to people God will not be merciful to him." (Bukhari and Muslim). RAS Vol 1, #227.

4) Anas Bin Malik relates that the Holy Prophet said: "No one of you becomes a true believer until he likes for his brother what he likes for himself." (Bukhari and Muslim). RAS Vol 1, #183.

5) Anas Bin Malik relates that the Holy Prophet said: "Help your brother, whether he is an oppressor or is oppressed. A man inquired, "O Messenger of God! I help him when he is oppressed, but how can I help him when he is an oppressor? He said, "You can keep him from committing oppression. That will be your help to him." (Bukhari). RAS Vol 1, #237.

6) Abu Hurairah relates that the Holy Prophet said: "Look at those who stand at a lower level than you but don't look at those who stand at a higher level than you, for this would make the favours (conferred upon you by God) insignificant (in your eyes)." (Muslim 42.7070).

7) Abdullah bin 'Amr bin Al-'Aas says that the Holy Prophet did not indulge in loose talk nor did he like to listen to it. He used to say, "The best of you is the best among you in conduct." (Bukhari and Muslim). RAS, Vol 1, #625.

8) Sahl bin Sa'd says that the Holy Prophet has said: "Whosoever gives me a guarantee to safeguard what is between his jaws [backbitting, lies, etc.] and what is between his legs [adultery, etc.], I shall guarantee him paradise." (Bukhari and Muslim). RAS Vol 2, #1513

9) Abu Hurairah relates that the Holy Prophet said: "The believers who show the most perfect faith are those who have the best behaviour, and the best of you are those who are the best to your wives." (Tirmidhi). RAS Vol 1, #278

10) Abu Zarr relates that the Holy Prophet said: "Do not belittle any good deed. Even meeting your brother with a cheerful face (is a good deed)." (Muslim). RAS Vol 1, #121.

11) Anas Bin Malik relates that the Holy Prophet said: "Make things easy and do not make them difficult, cheer people up by conveying glad tidings to them and do not repulse (them)." (Muslim). RAS Vol 1, #637

12) Ayesha relates that the Holy Prophet said: "Do not abuse the dead, for they have reached the result of what they have done. (e.g. facing the consequences of their deeds)" (Bukhari 8.76.523).

13) Abu Hurairah relates that the Holy Prophet said: "Beware of envy because envy consumes (destroys) virtues just as fire consumes firewood." (Abu Daud). RAS Vol2, #1569

14) Wasila bin Al-As-qa'a relates that the Holy Prophet said: "Do not express pleasure at the misfortune of a brother lest God should bestow mercy upon him and make you suffer from a misfortune." (Tirmidhi). RAS Vol 2, #1577

15) Ibn Mas'ud relates that the Holy Prophet once asked: "Who of you loves the wealth of your heir more than your own wealth?" The companions said: "O Messenger of God, there is none of us that loves his heir's wealth more than his own wealth. He said: "Then his wealth is that which he has sent forward (his good deeds credited for his afterlife) but that which he retains belongs to his heir. (Bukhari). RAS Vol 1, #545

16) Ayaz bin Himar relates that the Holy Prophet said: "God has revealed to me that you should humble yourselves to one another. One should neither hold himself above another nor transgress against another." (Muslim). RAS. Vol 1, #602

17) Abdullah bin Mas'ud relates that the Holy Prophet said: "A true believer does not taunt or curse or abuse or talk indecently." (Tirmidhi). RAS, Vol 2, #1734.

18) Abu Hurairah relates that the Holy Prophet said: "A believer must not hate a believing woman, if he dislikes one of her characteristics he will be

pleased with another." (Muslim). RAS Vol 1, #275

19) Abu Hurairah relates that the Holy Prophet said: "RIchness is not the abundance of wealth, rather it is in the richness of the heart." (Bukhari and Muslim). RAS Vol 1, #522. (See Also Muslim 5.2287).

20) On the authority of Abu Huraira, who said the Messenger of God said: "(Part of) the beauty of a man's Islam is to leave what does not concern him" (Tirmidhi). Nawawi #12.

21) On the authority of Abu Huraira, that the Messenger of God said: "He who believes in God and the Last Day should speak well or otherwise keep quiet. Also he who believes in God and the Last Day should honour his neighbor. And he who believes in God and the Last Day should honor his guest. " (Bukhari & Muslim). Nawawi #15.

22) On the authority of Abu Malik al-Harith ibn Asim al-Ash'ari , who said: the Messenger of God said: "... Prayers are divine light; charity is a proof; patience is light, and the Qur'an is an proof for or against you. Every man goes forth in the morning and in fact he is seller of his soul. He either sets it free (e.g. doing good) or destroys it (e.g. doing evil). (Muslim). Nawawi #23.

23) On the authority of Abu Huraira , who said: the Messenger of God said: "Charity is to be given for every joint of the human body (as a sign of gratitude to God) everyday the sun rises. To judge justly between two persons is regarded as charity, and to help a man ride his riding animal, or to lift his luggage on

to it, is also regarded as charity, and (saying) a good word is also charity, and every step taken on one's way to offer prayer is also charity and to remove a harmful thing from the way is also charity.
(Bukhari 4.52.232:& Muslim). See also Nawawi #26

24) On the authority of an-Nawwas ibn Sam'an that the Prophet said: "Righteousness is good conduct, and sin is what rankles in your mind and which you dislike people finding out" (Muslim). Nawawi #27.

Section III: Islam & Christianity

THREE TRAITS

And nearest among them in love to the believers you will find those who say, "We are Christians": because among these are men devoted to learning and men who have renounced the world, and they are not arrogant. And when they listen to the revelation received by the Messenger, you will see their eyes overflowing with tears, for they recognize the truth: they pray: "Our Lord! we believe; write us down among the witnesses. What cause can we have not to believe in God and the truth which has come to us, seeing that we long for our Lord to admit us to the company of the righteous?" And for this their prayer has God rewarded them with gardens, with rivers flowing underneath,- their eternal home. Such is the recompense of those who do good.

Quran

Similarities

11
Common Ground: Judaism, Christianity & Islam

By Jerald F. Dirks, M.Div., Psy.D.

INTRODUCTION:

It is important to appreciate the common ground that links together Islam, Christianity, and Judaism. Each of the three religions maintains that there is only one God. Each of the three claims the same historical legacy within the prophetic tradition. All three urge one to avoid evil and wickedness, for there will be a general resurrection and a Day of Judgment. Each of the three finds impressive common ground with the other two when it comes to certain aspects of ethical and spiritual teaching. Using the analogy of a tree, each of the three religions claims to be the one, true, vertical extension of a trunk of primary revelation, with the other two religions being seen as lateral branches that deviate from the true-verticality of the original trunk.

Let us proceed with some specific examples.

JESUS:

Both Islam and Christianity proclaim the angelic annunciation to Mary and the virgin birth of Jesus.

> Behold! the angels said: "O Mary! God gives you glad tidings of a word from Him: his name will be Christ Jesus "...She said: "O my Lord! How shall I have a son when no man has touched me?" He said: "Even so: God creates what He wills, when He has decreed a plan, He but says to it 'Be', and it is!" ... The similitude of Jesus before God is as that of Adam; He created him from dust, then said to him: "Be" and he was (Qur'an 3:45a, 47, 59).

While many passages in the *Qur'an* deal with the mission, ministry, and miracles of Jesus, *Qur'an* 3:49 provides the most succinct encapsulation. This single verse informs the reader that Jesus performed many miracles "by God's leave" (e.g., turning a clay figure of a bird into a living bird, healing the blind and the lepers, and quickening the dead) and that he declared "what you eat, and what you store." In addition, *Qur'an* 19:27-34 states that Jesus spoke during infancy, and *Qur'an* 5:46 reports that God gave Jesus a gospel containing "guidance and light, and confirmation of the law that had come before him."

The story of the clay birds and of Jesus speaking in infancy may be new to most Christians, but both stories appear in early Christian literature. *The First Gospel of the Infancy of Jesus Christ* 1:2 details Jesus speaking in infancy, while 15:6 of the same apocryphal gospel and 1:2-10 of *Thomas' Gospel of the Infancy of Jesus Christ* narrate the story of the clay birds coming to life. Further, the list of miracles given in *Qur'an* 3:49 appears to overlap quite comfortably with similar lists given in the *New Testament* gospels. For example, *Qur'an* 3:49 has Jesus saying:

...I heal those born blind, and the lepers, and I quicken the dead, by God's leave; and I let you know what you may eat, and what you should store in your houses. Surely in this is a sign for you, if you are truly believers.

Similarly, the *New Testament* gospels have Jesus saying:

Go your way, and tell John what things ye have seen and heard; how that the blind see, the lame walk, the lepers are cleansed, the deaf hear, the dead are raised, to the poor the gospel is preached (*Luke* 7:22; see also *Matthew* 11:4b-5).

Finally, Islam, like Christianity, maintains that there is yet a future role for Jesus prior to the Day of Judgment. In a remarkable similarity to Christian thought, numerous sayings of Prophet Muhammad (*Muslim* #293,6931-6934,7015,7023; *Abu Dawud* #4310, *Al-Bukhari* 3:425,656; 4:657,658) contribute to the Islamic perspective that Jesus will descend back to earth, slay the Antichrist, and establish an earthly rule.

There is a particularly dramatic *Old Testament* passage that many Christians interpret as referring to this coming Messianic reign.

> The wolf also shall dwell with the lamb, and the leopard shall lie down with the kid; and the calf and the young lion and the fatling together; and a little child shall lead them. And the cow and the bear shall feed; their young ones shall lie down together: and the lion shall eat straw like the ox. And the sucking child shall play on the hole of the asp, and the weaned child shall put his hand on the adder's den. They shall not hurt nor destroy in all my holy mountain; for the earth shall be full of the knowledge of the Lord, as the waters cover the sea (Isaiah 11:6-9).

The Messianic reign is described in remarkably similar terms in the following saying of Prophet Muhammad.

> During Jesus' reign, such security will exist that a camel will graze with the lion and the beast of prey with cows and sheep. Children will play with snakes, and none harm the other (*Musnad* 406:2).

MARY:

It is not only Jesus that occupies an honored position in Islam. His mother Maryam (Mary) also does. It may surprise some Christians to know there is a whole chapter in the *Qur'an* entitled Maryam. Muslims also believe Mary to be one of two best women of creation – the other one being Asiya, wife of the Pharaoh (*Sahih Muslim*, book 31).

ETHICAL AND SPIRITUAL TEACHING:

Islam, Christianity, and Judaism all stress that proper adherence to the divine revelation involves establishing a proper relationship with God and with one's fellow man. The first classical expression of this viewpoint can be found in the Biblical Ten Commandments as stated in *Exodus* 20:1-17 and *Deuteronomy* 5:1-22. Using the traditional Protestant method of counting them, these commandments may be summarized as: (1) you shall have no other gods before God; (2) you shall not make any graven images or idols; (3) you shall not take the name of the Lord, your God, in vain; (4) remember the Sabbath day and keep it holy; (5) honor your father and your mother; (6) you shall not murder; (7) you shall not commit adultery; (8) you shall not steal; (9) you shall not bear false witness; and (10) you shall not covet. These Ten Commandments serve as a basic underpinning of the Judaeo-Christian system of ethics and are reflected quite dramatically in the ethical teachings of the *Qur'an*.

Your Lord hath decreed that you worship none but Him, and that you be kind to parents. Whether one or both of them attain old age in thy life, do not say to them a word of contempt, nor repel them, but address them in terms of honor ... Nor come near to adultery; for it is a shameful (deed) and an evil, opening the road (to other evils). Nor take life—which God has made sacred—except for just cause ... Give full measure when you measure, and weigh with a balance that is straight; that is the most fitting and the most advantageous in the final determination...And in nowise covet those things in which God has bestowed His gifts more freely on some of you than on others (*Qur'an* 17:23, 32-33a, 35; 4:32a; 22:30).

Let us pause for a moment to consider these Qur'anic injunctions. 1) "Your Lord hath decreed that you worship none but Him" You shall have no other gods before God. 2) "be kind to parents. Whether one or both of them attain old age in your life, do not say to them a word of contempt, nor repel them, but address them in terms of honor" Honor your father and your mother. 3) "Nor come near to adultery; for it is a shameful (deed) and an evil, opening the road (to other evils)." You shall not commit adultery. 4) "Nor take life—which God has made sacred—except for just cause" You shall not murder. 5) "Give full measure when you measure, and weigh with a balance that is straight" You shall not steal. 6) "And in nowise covet those things in which God has bestowed His gifts more freely on some of you than on others" You shall not covet.

As to the remaining four moral injunctions of the

Ten Commandments, one can easily find Qur'anic parallels to three of them. You shall not make any graven images or idols is consistent with Islam's traditional avoidance of creating artistic likenesses of any living creature and with the following Qur'anic injunction.

... shun the abomination of idols (*Qur'an* 22:30).

You shall not take the name of the Lord, your God, in vain is paralleled by *Qur'an* 24:53.

They swear their strongest oaths by God that, if only you would command them, they would leave (their homes). Say: "Do not swear; obedience is (more) reasonable; verily, God is well acquainted with all that you do."

You shall not bear false witness finds expression in many passages of the *Qur'an* (e.g., 2:42; 4:112; 25:72-75; 40:28; 45:27; 51:10; 56:92; and 58:14-15), but is perhaps expressed best in *Qur'an* 2:42 and 51:10.

And do not cover truth with falsehood, nor conceal the truth when you know (what it is)...Woe to the falsehood mongers.

Thus, only the Decalogue's injunction to remember the Sabbath day is not to be found in Islam.

A second fundamental ethical precept of the *Old Testament* is the Lex Talionis (law of retaliation in kind) found in the so-called Mosaic Law.

> And if any mischief follow, then thou shalt give life for life, eye for eye, tooth for tooth, hand for hand, foot for foot, burning for burning, wound for wound, stripe for stripe. (*Exodus* 21:23-25)

Of note, the *New Testament* claims that Jesus modified this Lex Talionis when he reportedly said:

> Ye have heard that it hath been said, An eye for an eye, and a tooth for a tooth: but I say unto you, that ye resist not evil: but whosoever shall smite thee on thy right cheek, turn to him the other also. (*Matthew* 5:38-39; see also *Luke* 6:29)

In the above verses, Jesus reportedly suggests that the Lex Talionis should be softened with charity, mercy, and forgiveness. This call for a compassionate modification of the Lex Talionis is also found in the Qur'an.

> We ordained therein for them: "Life for life, an eye for an eye, nose for nose, ear for ear, tooth for tooth, and wounds equal for equal." But if anyone remits the retaliation by way of charity, it is an act of atonement for himself... (*Qur'an* 5:45)

Let us consider another of the great ethical teachings

attributed to Jesus in the *New Testament*, one that dramatically illustrates our social duty and responsibility to our fellow man.

Then shall he say also unto them on the left hand. Depart from me ye cursed into everlasting fire, prepared for the devil and his angels: for I was an hungred, and ye gave me no meat: I was thirsty, and ye gave me no drink: I was a stranger, and ye took me not in: naked, and ye clothed me not: sick, and in prison, and ye visited me not. Then shall they also answer him, saying, Lord, when saw we thee an hungred, or athirst, or a stranger, or naked, or sick, or in prison, and did not minister unto thee? Then shall he answer them, saying, verily I say unto you, inasmuch as ye did it not to one of the least of these, ye did it not to me. And these shall go away into everlasting punishment: but the righteous into life eternal.   (*Matthew* 25:41-46)

Islam offers an almost identical ethical instruction, which is found in the sayings of Prophet Muhammad.

God's Apostle said: "Verily, God, the exalted and glorious, will say on the Day of Resurrection: 'O son of Adam, I was sick but you did not visit Me.' He will say: 'O my Lord, how could I visit You when You are the Lord of the worlds?' Thereupon He will say: 'Didn't you know that a certain servant of Mine was sick, but you did not visit him, and were you not aware that if you had visited him, you would have found Me by him? O son of Adam, I asked you for food but you did not feed Me.' He will say: 'My Lord, how could I feed

You when You are the Lord of the worlds?' He will say: 'Did you not know that a certain servant of Mine asked you for food but you did not feed him, and were you not aware that if you had fed him you would have found him by My side?' (The Lord will again say:) 'O son of Adam, I asked you for something to drink, but you did not provide Me with any.' He will say: 'My Lord, how could I provide You with something to drink when You are the Lord of the worlds?' Thereupon, He will say: 'A certain servant of Mine asked you for a drink but you did not provide him with one, and had you provided him with a drink you would have found him near Me'" (*Muslim, Hadith #6232*).

In another passage, the *New Testament* reports that Jesus warned his followers against false piety in giving alms, stressed that one's heavenly reward is based upon one's intentions as much as one's behavior, and suggested that one's acts of charity should not be made public.

Take heed that ye do not your alms before men, to be seen of them: otherwise ye have no reward of your Father which is in heaven. Therefore when thou doest thine alms, do not sound a trumpet before thee, as the hypocrites do in the synagogues and in the streets, that they may have glory of men. Verily I say unto you, they have their reward. But when thou doest alms, let not thy left hand know what thy right hand doeth; that thine alms may be in secret: and thy Father which seeth in secret Himself shall reward thee openly. (*Matthew* 6:1-4)

The following passage from the *Qur'an* appears to be a direct parallel.

> O ye who believe! Do not cancel your charity by reminders of your generosity or by injury—like those who spend their substance to be seen of men, but believe neither in God nor in the Last Day (*Qur'an* 2:264a).

Before leaving our consideration of *Matthew* 6:1-4, it may be helpful to quote an example from the sayings of Prophet Muhammad, one which parallels the reported words of Jesus regarding the proper way of giving alms.

> God's Messenger said: "When God created the earth... the angels ... asked if anything in His (God's) creation was stronger than wind, and He replied, 'Yes, the son of Adam who gives charity with his right hand while concealing it from his left.'" (*Al-Tirmidhi, Hadith #192*)

The *New Testament* states that Jesus also warned against false piety in the performance of prayers.

> And when thou prayest, thou shalt not be as the hypocrites are: for they love to pray standing in the synagogues and in the corners of the streets, that they may be seen of men. Verily I say unto you, they have their reward. But thou, when thou prayest, enter into thy closet, and when thou hast shut thy door, pray to thy Father which is in secret; and thy Father which seeth in secret shall reward thee openly. But when ye pray, use not vain repetitions, as the heathen do: for thy

think that they shall be heard for their much speaking. (*Matthew* 6:5-7)

Similar sentiments are expressed in *Qur'an* 107:4-7.

So woe to the worshippers who are neglectful of their prayers, those who (want only) to be seen (by man), but refuse (to supply even) neighborly needs.

The ethical considerations stated in *Matthew* 6:5-7 also find clear and unambiguous expression in a saying of Prophet Muhammad, wherein he implied that the Antichrist was less of a threat to a believer than was the believer who altered his prayer out of false piety.

God's Messenger came out to them when they were discussing the Antichrist, and asked if they would like him to tell what caused him more fear for them than the Antichrist. They replied that they certainly would, so he said, "Latent polytheism, meaning that a man will stand up and pray and lengthen his prayer because he sees someone looking at him" (*Al-Tirmidhi, Hadith #5333*).

For many Christians, the pinnacle of the reported ethical instruction of Jesus can be found in the so-called Golden Rule.

Therefore all things whatsoever ye would that men

should do to you, do ye even so to them: for this is the law and the prophets. (Matthew 7:12; see also Luke 6:31)

Variations on the Golden Rule can also be found in prior Jewish writings. For example, a precursor to the Golden Rule is attributed to Rabbi Hillel, in which he instructed that one should not do to others what one would not want done to oneself. An additional Jewish precursor to the Golden Rule can be identified in the *Old Testament* apocryphal writings.

And what you hate, do to no man. (*Tobit* 4:14)

The Islamic parallel to the Golden Rule can be found in the teachings of Prophet Muhammad.

The Prophet said: "None of you will have faith until he wishes for his brother what he likes for himself." (*Al-Bukhari*, Hadith #1:12)

Consider one final example of the commonality to be found between Islam and the Judaeo-Christian tradition. The author of the *Epistle of James* warns man against taking himself too seriously.

Go to now, ye that say, to day or tomorrow we will go into such a city, and continue there a year, and buy and sell, and get gain: whereas ye know not what shall be on the morrow. For what is your life? It is even a vapour, that appeareth for a little time, and then vanisheth away. For that ye ought to say, if the Lord will, we shall live, and do this, or that. (*James* 4:13-15)

The *Qur'an* also warns against this type of arrogance.

Nor say of anything, "I shall be sure to do so and so tomorrow,"without adding, "So please God!" (*Qur'an* 18:23-24a).

SUMMARY AND CONCLUSIONS:

Despite the impressive consensus that is to be found among the three Abrahamic faiths, it must be acknowledged that there are also very real differences among them. Among these fundamental differences that divide the Abrahamic faiths, one can list the following issues: 1) the divine mission and ministry of Jesus Christ—universal according to contemporary Christianity, specific to the children of Israel according to Islam, and non-existent according to Judaism; 2) the alleged crucifixion of Jesus—reality according to contemporary Christianity and Judaism, illusion according to Islam; 3) the nature of Jesus—divinity according to contemporary Christianity, humanity according to Islam and Judaism; and 4) the nature of God—trinity according to contemporary Christianity, unity according to Islam and Judaism. Additional disagreements among the Abrahamic faiths concern the status of Muhammad as a prophet of God, the status of the contemporary *Bible* as divine revelation, and the status of the *Qur'an* as divine revelation.

These differences, however, should not obscure the equally real and equally important similarities in religious history, heritage, and core beliefs that are to be found among the three Abrahamic faiths. Nor should these differences blind us to the fact that Jews, Christians, and Muslims share a common core of religious values, a common embrace of religious idealism, and a common religious belief in their social obligations and duties to their fellow man.

Compiler's Note: If you liked this chapter, why not surf over to a fun quiz inspired by this material, at the book website.

www.EasilyUnderstandIslam.com/islam-christianity-quiz.html

It a unique way to introduce friends to the concepts in this chapter which they should enjoy and remember. Check it out.

Differences

We understand that this is a sensitive subject for some readers. To put this in context, please read the previous section on the deep love and respect Muslims have for many things that Christians hold dear. For example, the extraordinary level of love and respect towards Jesus is an article of faith in Islam. This does not exist in any other religion outside of Christianity and Islam. But, there are differences. In so far as possible, we have attempted to present this section in a responsible and logical, instead of in an emotional, manner. We have tried to focus honestly on core issues instead of on distracting peripheral ones. We have endeavored to use meaningful standard sources and objective techniques.

Since these are core questions and issues – some of which, in one form or another, have spanned human history — we believe they need to be explored. Finally, we do recognize that there are individuals who feel that they have found fulfillment and been lifted up by their religion. And we explicitly acknowledge that there are many individuals who are good people trying their best to do the right thing. We do not seek to deny their feelings, but simply wish to present different perspectives.

Of course, differences do not preclude cooperation and friendship. Individuals can (without comprising their essential beliefs) find common goals with people outside their faith traditions to strive together on issues of compassion, justice and truth.

Note: Muslims' views of Christianity are based on the Quran

and the example of the Prophet as understood by Muslim scholars. Muslims do not base their beliefs on the Bible since Muslims believe it no longer accurately reflects God's original revelation although it may well contain significant traces of that revelation. In the interests of understanding, we provide a possible way that some Muslims might view or highlight certain passages and messages in the Bible which may well be different from the way the reader may have previously viewed certain verses.

The Prophet said, "God says: 'I am just as My servant thinks I am, and I am with him if He remembers Me. If he remembers Me himself, I too, remember him Myself; and if he remembers Me in a group of people, I remember him in a group that is better than that; and if he comes one span nearer to Me, I go one cubit nearer to him; and if he comes one cubit nearer to Me, I go a distance of two outstretched arms nearer to him; and if he comes to Me walking, I go to him running.'
(Sahih Buhkari Volume 9, Book 93, Number 502)

Abu Huraira reported God's Messenger as saying: "None among you can get into Paradise by virtue of your deeds alone." They said:,"God's Messenger, not even you?" Thereupon he said, "Not even I, but that God should wrap me in His Grace and Mercy." (Sahih Muslim book 039, number 6764)

Note: Escaping hell and gaining paradise is such an enormous reward that our paltry good deeds ALONE (however great) are insufficient to justify it. But the Grace and Mercy of God is extraordinary.

The Bible and the Word of God

By Jerald F. Dirks, M.Div., Psy.D.

INTRODUCTION

If the *Bible* is the literal word of God, then God frequently contradicts Himself, makes mistakes that He later regrets, and has a poor grasp of dates and history. For those unwilling to accept the above description of God, a group that includes all Muslims, the conclusion is obvious. The *Bible*, as it currently exists, is not the word of God, although it may be a corrupted version of what once was the word of God. While the above may appear to be highly provocative statements, a little Biblical detective work provides the necessary proof to support the charges.

CONTRADICTIONS IN THE BIBLE

It is impossible to present all of the instances in which the *Bible* is self-contradictory within the short confines of this chapter. The following examples should suffice, however, to illustrate how self-contradictory the *Bible* actually is.

Can we see God? *Exodus* 33:20 and *John* 1:18 clearly state that no one has ever seen God and that no one can see God and still live. Yet, *Genesis* 32:30, *Exodus* 24:10, *Job* 42:5, and *Isaiah* 6:1 all proclaim that people have seen God and lived to tell about it.

What was the genealogy of Jesus Christ? In an implied refutation of the virgin birth of Jesus (both Muslims and Christians proclaim the virgin birth of Jesus), *Matthew* 1:1-16 and *Luke* 3:23-38 both trace Christ's genealogy through Joseph, the reported husband of the Virgin Mary. Even more alarming, the two genealogies are in total disagreement with each other concerning the ancestry of Joseph, with *Matthew* saying that Jacob was the father of Joseph and *Luke* saying that it was Heli. If that weren't enough, *I Chronicles* 2:1-15 contradicts *Matthew*'s account of the generations between Uzziah (Ahaziah) and Jotham by adding three generations (Joash, Amaziah, and Azariah) between the two. Further, *I Chronicles* adds the name of Jehoiakim between those of Josiah and Jechoniah. So, who is right concerning the father of Joseph? Is it *Matthew* or *Luke*? If *Matthew* is right, who is right concerning the extended genealogy? Is it *Matthew* or *I Chronicles*? If the *Bible* is the word of God, how could God have gotten so confused?

If the *Bible* is the word of God, why are there major counting irregularities?. In summing up the genealogy listed in *Matthew* 1:1-16, *Matthew* 1:17 says that there were 14 generations from Abraham to David, 14 generations from David to the deportation, and 14 generations from the deportation to Jesus

Christ. A simple count of the generations provided by *Matthew* between Abraham and David and between Solomon and Jechoniah reveals 14 generations, but the count between Salathiel and Jesus is only 13 generations. [1]

A second counting problem occurs in *Matthew* 12:38-40. In referring to the alleged crucifixion and resurrection of Jesus, the passage indicates that Jesus would spend "three days and three nights in the heart of the earth." But, if Jesus were crucified on Good Friday and arose on Easter Sunday, concepts rejected by Islam, there is simply no way that he could spend "three nights in the heart of the earth." At most, one has Friday and Saturday nights, and one plus one does not equal three.

There are numerous other number problems that occur in the *Bible*, as illustrated by the following examples. 1) Did David take seven hundred horsemen (*II Samuel* 8:3-4) captive from King Hadadezer of Zobah or seven thousand (*I Chronicles* 18:3-4)? 2) *II Samuel* 24:9 says that 800,000 men of Israel "drew the sword," while *I Chronicles* 21:5 pegs the number at 100,000. (Other number discrepancies can be found between *II Samuel* 24:9 and *I Chronicles* 21:5.) 3) Did Solomon have 3,300 (*I Kings* 5:15-16) supervisors for his conscripted workforce or 3,600 (*II Chronicles* 2:2)? 4) Did Hiram, the bronze worker, make for the Solomonic Temple 2,000 baths (*I Kings* 7:26) or 3,000 (*II Chronicles* 4:5)? 5) Did two blind men (*Matthew* 20:30-34) beseech Jesus for healing of their eyes, or was it only one (*Mark* 10:46-52)? 6) In fighting the Syrians (Arameans), did David kill the men of 700 chariots (*II Samuel* 10:18) or 7,000 men who fought in chariots (*I Chronicles* 19:18)? The two numbers are mutually exclusive, as there was simply not enough room in a chariot to have 10 men per chariot; the typical number was three, as demonstrated in the figures of 4,000 chariots and 12,000 horsemen given in *II Chronicles* 9:25. 7) Were there 200 singers (*Ezra* 2:65) among the returning Israelite exiles or 245 (*Nehemiah* 7:67)?

Are "cavalry" and "infantry" the same? *II Samuel* 10:18 says that David killed 40,000 "horsemen" of Syria (Aramea) while *I Chronicles* 19:18 says it was 40,000 "footmen."

How many children did Michal, the daughter of King Saul, actually have? *II Samuel* 6:23 states that Michal "had no child unto the day of her death." But, *II Samuel* 21:8 credits her with having five sons. Which "word of God" are we to believe?

How did Judas Iscariot, the disciple who reportedly betrayed Jesus, actually die? *Matthew* 27:5 states that Judas committed suicide by hanging, while *Acts* 1:18 says that Judas disemboweled himself when he fell. If both passages are the word of God, how could God contradict Himself in such a blatant manner?

To this point, we have been confining our exploration of contradictions in the *Bible* to those found primarily by comparing one passage with another. However, there are also internal contradictions within a single passage. For example, was Joseph made captive and taken to Egypt by Ishmaelites (the descendants of Abraham's son, Ishmael) who had purchased Joseph from his brothers or by Midianites (the descendants of Abraham's son, Midian) who had pulled Joseph out of a pit? *Genesis* 37:12-36 swings back and forth in a seemingly unending stream of contradictions in attempting to answer these questions.

As a second example of internal contradiction within a single Biblical passage, consider *Genesis* 22:1-13. This passage states that the son Abraham was to sacrifice was "Isaac" and Abraham's "only son". Now, *Genesis* 16:15-16 states that Ishmael was born when Abraham was 84 years old, *Genesis* 21:5 claims that Isaac was born when Abraham was 100 years old, and *Genesis* 25:7-11 maintains that Ishmael was still alive at the time of Abraham's death. Therefore, the only time Abraham had an only son was after the birth of Ishmael and before the birth of Isaac, making Ishmael, not Isaac, the intended sacrificial victim. (Attempts to resolve this contradiction by translating the Hebrew word *yachiyd* as "beloved," as some versions of the *Bible* do, are specious. *Yachiyd* means "sole" or "only," and it is only by being the "sole" or "only" that the word "beloved" can be implied.)

DOES GOD MAKE MISTAKES?

Almost all monotheists, whether Jews, Christians, or Muslims, would agree that God is perfect, which implies that God cannot make mistakes that he later regrets. Yet, *Genesis* 6:5-6 states that God regretted His having created mankind. This passage is so explicit in stating that God had erred and regretted his prior creation and so poignant in describing God's grief over His mistake that it is worth quoting the verses in their entirety.

And God saw that the wickedness of man was great in the earth, and that every imagination of the thoughts of his heart was only evil continually, and it repented the Lord that he had made man on the earth, and it grieved him at his heart.

If we accept this passage as the word of God, then God has told us that He makes mistakes, lacks foreknowledge of what will later transpire, and regrets and grieves over His prior mistakes. Such a picture of God is far from God being perfect in every way and is a portrayal that no Muslim can accept.

GOD AND HISTORY

Genesis 39:1-50:7 typically refers to the ruler(s) of Egypt at the time of Joseph, the son of Jacob, as being "pharaoh" (*per-o*, meaning "the great house"). In marked contrast, *Qur'an* 12:43-76 consistently refers to Prophet Yusuf's Egyptian monarch as being a "king" (*Al-Malik*) and not a "pharaoh." This is so even though the *Qur'an* parallels the *Bible* in referring to the ruler of Egypt at the time of Moses as being "pharaoh" (*Fir'aun* or *Al-Fir'aun*), not as "king" [2].

The title "pharaoh" came into common use in ancient Egypt about the beginning of the 18th Dynasty [3]. According to the conventional chronology for ancient Egypt, the 18th Dynasty began circa 1,539 BCE, which suggests that the title "pharaoh" was in use by that time, but not much earlier than that. As such, *Genesis* appears to be placing Joseph after 1,539 BCE, an impossibly late date according to the *Bible*'s own chronology. (Almost all Biblical scholars place the start of the Solomonic Temple at around

966 BCE. *I Kings* 6:1 says that Israelite exodus from Egypt began 480 years prior to the start of the Solomonic Temple, i.e., circa 1446 BCE. Further, *Exodus* 12:40 says that the Israelites toiled in Egypt for 430 years, which would place the start of Joseph's time in Egypt no later than 1876 BCE.)

So, why does God incorrectly refer to the ruler of Joseph's Egypt as "pharaoh" in the *Bible* but correctly as "king" in the *Qur'an*? Is God guilty of committing historical anachronisms? If the *Bible* is the word of God, the *Bible* would appear to say He is.

As a second example of the *Bible* being in conflict with known history, consider the birth of Jesus Christ. According to *Matthew* 2:1-21, Jesus was born when Herod was king of Judea. This places the birth of Jesus at 4 BCE at the very latest, because Herod the Great, the only Herod to hold the title of King of Judea, died in 4 BCE. But, *Luke* 2:1-7 argues that Jesus was born during a universal census when Quirinius was governor of Syria. It is a point of historical fact that there was no universal census within the Roman Empire at this time. Now, there was a Palestinian census when Publius Sulpicius Quirinius was governor. But neither the Palestinian census nor the governorship of Quirinius existed prior to 6 CE, a discrepancy of at least 10 years with the account in *Matthew*.

THE FORMATION OF THE BIBLE:

How can one begin to explain the numerous contradictions within the *Bible*? How can the *Bible* be at variance with known history? The answers lie in understanding how the *Bible* was created.

The *Bible* as we currently know it evolved over the course of well over 1,000 years, and was frequently a cut-and-paste compilation from earlier and often discrepant sources. Along the way, different versions of the *Bible* emerged.

As an example, consider the *Torah* or Pentateuch, which is comprised of *Genesis*, *Exodus*, *Leviticus*, *Numbers*, and *Deuteronomy*. Modern Biblical scholars have ascertained that these books are a cut-and-paste compilation from earlier written sources known as J, E, D, and P. The oldest of these sources, i.e., J, dates only to about 950 BCE. The newest of these sources, i.e., P, was composed during the fifth and sixth centuries BCE. Around 400 BCE, enterprising Jewish scribes combined these four sources and other unidentified material to create the *Torah*. Over the next few centuries, several different versions of the *Torah* emerged, including: the Palestinian text (fragments of which have been found among the Dead Sea Scrolls); the proto-Masoretic text (the text upon which the current Masoretic text used by Jews is based); the Alexandrian text (the text upon which the Greek *Septuagint* is based); and the Samaritan text (the text still used by a small group of existing Samaritans). The modern English translations of *Genesis*, *Exodus*, *Leviticus*, *Numbers*, and *Deuteronomy* are based on the work of Biblical scholars who make use of all four texts, variously choosing this one or that one, based upon linguistic, historical, and "best guess" considerations. Yet, the differences that exist among these ancient texts can be illustrated by the fact that the Masoretic and

Samaritan texts differ in some 6,000 places, with the Samaritan text agreeing with the *Septuagint* in about 1/3 of those places! Which text is to be believed?

After about 300 BCE, some consensus had arisen among the Greek-speaking Jews in Alexandria about which books belonged in the canonical scripture, giving rise to the Greek Septuagint as their authoritative book of scripture. But, the final decision on which books would comprise the canonical Jewish scriptures or *Old Testament* was not arrived at until the Council of Jamnia circa 90 CE. This gave rise to the *Septuagint* and the Masoretic text having two different sets of books included in them, most of which overlapped with each other, but some of which existed only in the *Septuagint*. Generally speaking, contemporary Roman Catholics follow the *Septuagint* while modern Protestants follow the Masoretic text, explaining why the so-called Roman Catholic *Bible* has additional books, known as the Apocrypha, which are not found in the so-called Protestant *Bible*.

Well, what about the *New Testament*? The 27 books comprising the *New Testament* represent those books of scripture that are exclusive to Christianity. Of these 27 books, one is an apocalypse (*Revelation*), one is an early church history (*Acts*), 21 are epistles of one sort or another, and four are labeled as being gospels (*Matthew*, *Mark*, *Luke*, and *John*). It is highly doubtful that any of these 27 books was written by anyone who had first-hand contact with Jesus.

The canon of the *New Testament* evolved gradually over several centuries. During the first three centuries of the so-called Christian era, there was no concept of an authorized and closed canon of *New Testament* scripture. Various books were viewed as scriptural based upon their self-stated claim to being inspired and based upon their circulation and popularity among the various Christian churches. As such, what was regarded as scripture in one locality was not regarded as scripture in another locality. But, early in the fourth century, the situation began to change. In his *Ecclesiastical History*, Eusebius Pamphili, the fourth century bishop of Caesarea, proposed a canon of *New Testament* scripture. Of significance, this proposed canon omitted many books currently found in the *New Testament*, including *James*, *Jude*, *II Peter*, *II John*, *III John*, and *Revelation*. In 367, Athanasius, the bishop of Alexandria, circulated an Easter letter, which included the first listing of *New Testament* scripture to conform exactly to the current *New Testament*, although only a few years before he had still been championing *The Shepherd of Hermas* as being canonical scripture. This canon of *New Testament* scripture was later ratified at the Council of Hippo in 393, the Synod of Carthage in 397, and the Carthaginian Council in 419. But, there was not agreement with this proposed canon among the so-called Eastern churches until the sixth century, when the Syriac translation of circa 508 CE finally conformed to this canon.

As can be seen, it took three to five centuries after the completion of the ministry of Jesus before the early Christian churches had arrived at a closed canon of the 27 books presently comprising the *New Testament*. Along the way, the selection process was constantly being influenced by human, political, geographical, and theological considerations that had precious little to do with preserving the word of God. As an example, only four gospels found their way into the *New Testament.* However, over 40 gospels were known to have existed and to have been accepted as authoritative scripture by one or another of the early Christian churches. Additionally, examination of some of the earliest texts of these *New Testament* books reveals that editorial changes were being made in the texts throughout the early centuries of Christianity.

CONCLUSIONS

Does God contradict Himself, make errors in judgment that He later regrets, and make mistakes regarding the known historical record? Of course He does not. But men are highly fallible, and men do contradict themselves and make historical mistakes. As seen above, the formation of the *Bible* took place over a millennium of time. Editing and selection decisions were frequently based on human, political, and churchly considerations that trumped spiritual truth. Along the way, the literal word of God was slowly lost, and the reader of the contemporary *Bible* is left to sift through countless contradictions and historical impossibilities.

Notes:

[1] Some might insist that *Matthew* said 14 generations from the deportation to Jesus, so Jechoniah should be counted as the 14th generation in the second set and as the first generation in the third set, resulting in 14 generations in the third set. If that were the

case, however, then David should be counted as both the 14th generation in the first set and as the first generation in the second set, resulting in 15 generations in the second set. There is just no way to make the math work out.

[2] *Qur'an* 2:49; 7:103-104, 109, 113, 123, 130, 137; 8:54; 10:75, 79, 83, 88, 90; 11:97; 14:6; 17:101-102; 20:24, 43, 60, 78-79; 23:46; 26:11, 16, 23, 41, 44, 53; 27:12; 28:3-4, 6, 8-9, 32, 38; 29:39; 40:24, 26, 28-29, 36-37, 45-46; 43:46, 51; 51:38; and 79:17.

[3] Laughlin JCH: Pharaoh. In Mills WE et al. (eds): *Mercer Dictionary of the Bible.* Macon, Mercer University Press, 1997. Page 679.

13

The Bible & Modern Science

By F. Kamal

This is an examination of the Bible and modern science focusing on three selected topics: The order of creation, the dates of creation, and Noah's flood.

GENESIS DETAILS THE BIBLICAL ORDER OF CREATION

(Rough Chronology according to Genesis Chapter One)

SYNPOSIS

This lists the sequence of creation according to the Bible:

First Day: There was a formless void of earth and heaven, darkness and water. God then created light.

Second Day: The firmament (e.g. arch/expanse of sky, heavens) was built. The water (e.g. rain) was separated from the water (e.g. ocean) by the firmament.

Third Day: Earth appears as waters grouped into

seas. Earthly vegetation and fruits appear.

Fourth Day: Sun, stars, moon are set up as "lights" in the firmament (Gen 1:16).

Fifth Day: Winged fowls, great whales, "the waters brought forth" moving creatures

Sixth Day: Cattle, creeping things, beasts of the earth. Finally man.

DIFFICULTIES

1) Genesis places water as existing at the beginning -- even before light and stars (Gen 1:2,3,5,16,19). Current scientific thought postulates the creation of water, composed of a fairly complex molecule, much later in the creation. [1]

2) The earth and earthly vegetation bearing fruits (Gen 1:12,13) appear on day three before the stars, sun, and moon (Gen 1:16, 19) appear on the fourth day. Plant like organisms have indeed recently been discovered in very deep (e.g., light deprived) oceans possibly subsisting via thermal/volcanic nutrition. But, earthly fruit bearing vegetables as described in Genesis are unlikely to have survived without sunlight (especially if the days are not 24 hour days, but long periods) -- although it is conceded that "light" and "darkness" might sustain them "somehow." Modern science currently believes the stars, sun, and moon developed before vegetation and fruits on earth. The formed earth is not believed to have independently existed in a time before the formed sun, moon, and stars as described in Genesis. Our own solar system

is believed to have formed around the same time scale and with substantially the same source material.

3) There is a contradiction in Genesis about the order of creation, Genesis 2:5-9 ("J" strand or the Yahwist source) appears to strongly imply man's creation before vegetation (which would contradict modern science). Other Genesis passages (Gen 1:12,13,16,19; "P" strand) place vegetation before man (which is in agreement with current scientific knowledge). Science, based on the layering of index fossils in sedimentary strata, indicates that man's creation occurred long after the creation of plants.

CREATION DATES

BIBLICAL CHRONOLOGY

Analysis of Genesis and the genealogies in Luke and Mark, along with the other chronological markers mentioned in the Bible, compared with well known secular records such as the building of the first temple around 965 BCE can be used to establish the dates of creation. [2] This can be juxtaposed against current scientific knowledge for purposes of elucidation, criticism, and commentary.

BIBLICAL TIMELINE

According to Genesis, man (e.g. Adam, [3]) appears on the sixth day of creation [4]. Further, Genesis allows one to date Abraham around 2000 years after Adam.[5] Biblical scholars using similar techniques place Abraham around twenty centuries before

Christ. [6] Creation is therefore placed around 4000 BCE or around 6000 years ago. [7]

CURRENT SCIENTIFIC THOUGHT
(A sampling of "clocks")

BIOLOGICAL ESTIMATES

Genetic dating techniques, suggest that an "Eve" would have lived at least 6,500 years ago. Exact time estimates for "Eve" (or a possible age of humans) vary based on models and assumptions and may be different from each other. [8] This technique analyzed mitochondrial DNA variations among an ethnically diverse group of individuals. (Mitochondrial DNA — unlike nucleic DNA — is only inherited from one's mother, who herself inherited it from her mother, who inherited from her mother, back to a common maternal ancestor). If there were no mutation, everyone in the sampled population's mitochondrial DNA would be the same (e.g. from Eve), but it does mutate. Assuming a fairly constant mutation rate to account for the diversity in the sample group, [9] an extrapolated time for a common maternal ancestor is suggested. [10][11]

GEOLOGY

Ice cores are similar to tree rings. Analysis of ice cores shows at least 30,000 "summer and winter bands" suggesting a lower bound of at least 30,000 years for the age of the earth. [12]

PHYSICS ESTIMATES

Radiometric dating techniques used to establish age of the solar system: Radiometric dating exploits the decay of radioactive isotopes over periods called half–lives to record the passage of time. Using various isotope methods (Ar-Ar, Rb-Sr, Sm-Nd) on many different meteorites, a lower bound for the date of the solar system has been put at around 4.5 billion years. [13] (Note: The solar system itself formed fairly long after the universe came into being.)

Star Evolution Models: The gobular clusters contain the oldest stars in the galaxy. Using star evolution models to study them, scientists date these stars in the order of 11-18 billion years old, placing some possible bounds on the age of the universe.

Big Bang Model: This model is used to explain the recession of all galaxies around us (e.g. redshift), background radiation in all directions, and helps explain Einstein's nonstatic theory of general relativity. If one "rewinds" the Big Bang explosion from its current state to the initial singularity, an estimate of the age of the universe emerges. This estimate can still vary based on the measured density/geometry of the universe (e.g. is it flat?) to things like its actual composition (e.g. amount of matter, "dark cold matter", "dark energy", etc.) .

WMAP Satellite data: The most current estimate of the age of the universe is provided by new data from the WMAP Satellite. This suggests an age of 13.7 billion years. [14]

CONCLUSION ON DATES

Due to constraints of space, we have only sampled a few main ideas in modern science, yet there appear to be clear difficulties between current modern mainstream science and a literal view of the Bible.

GLOBAL FLOOD (NOAH)

Genesis 6-8 talks about a global flood (e.g. Genesis 6:5-8, Genesis 7:19-23, Genesis 8:9, Genesis 9:12) survived by Noah and the inhabitants of his ark. Furthermore, Biblical markers can also place this flood around Noah's 600th year (Genesis 7:6) or most probably around 2200-2500 BCE.

> From Genesis 7:19-24: And the waters prevailed exceedingly upon the earth; and all the high hills, that were under the whole heaven, were covered. Fifteen cubits upward did the waters prevail; and the mountains were covered. And all flesh died that moved upon the earth, both of fowl, and of cattle, and of beast, and of every creeping thing that creepeth upon the earth, and every man: All in whose nostrils was the breath of life, of all that was in the dry land, died. And every living substance was destroyed which was upon the face of the ground, both man, and cattle, and the creeping things, and the fowl of the heaven; and they were destroyed from the earth: and Noah only remained alive, and they that were with him in the ark. And the waters prevailed upon the earth an hundred and fifty days.

Two important points can be gleaned from the Genesis account: 1) It was a massive global flood;

and 2) All living substance perished on earth except what was on the ark. [15]

One wonders the obvious: How were the small crew of Noah able to collect, maintain, and contain samples of all the world's creatures and fowl in an ark only 450 feet long, 75 feet wide and 45 feet high (Genesis 6:15) without the use of miracles?

There are even questions relating to the period after the flood receded. Since the species were taken on in pairs (approximately), how did the herbivores survive with such a lopsided ratio of the predators (e.g. lions, tigers, etc.) to herbivores without the world's entire food chain rapidly collapsing very soon after the flood? Normally, the food web hierarchy is displayed as a sharp pyramid (e.g., ratio of herbivores to predators is huge).

Archeologists have found evidence of local floods, the most well known perhaps being Woolley's discovery in Mesopotamia (Ur). While it is difficult to say with certainty that this was "Noah's flood," the excavation does show specific clues. For example, the Ur bed or strata contained sand *with tiny marine fragments* embedded in the mud and was a massive 10 feet deep. The styles in pottery were markedly different in the strata above and below it. But, the Mesopotamia flood was a local, not global flood. A global flood should have left a massive trace in the earth's geological record, which has still not been revealed.

CAUTIONS

Science attempts to build models. Good scientific models explain data (including new data) better than models they replace, make verifiable predictions, and hopefully limit assumptions/axioms to that with which one may feel comfortable. Because of these reasons, for example, as new datum emerges, or assumptions are challenged, models may evolve --although normally not dramatically. Hence science can be said — in a sense — to be "in flux," and limited to (directly or indirectly) measurable data. Unfortunately, this dependence on the quality of the data reminds one of the old adage: "Garbage in, garbage out." In other words, if the data and/or assumptions are bad, the analysis will be flawed.

To use an overly simplistic *imagined* experiment, let us consider the earth. In olden days, due to our poor localized data (e.g. measuring abilities limited primarily to intuitive rough guesses with our eyesight) we might have concluded the world is flat. But today, we can take photographs of earth from space. The new data cannot sustain old conclusions. The world is clearly not flat. A paradigm shift would occur in this imagined set of experiments.

Because the horizons of science are constantly being redefined and because science is limited to measurable observations, science is probably ultimately better as a confirmer of something that is a truth than as an "undisputable disprover" of an alleged truth – even if the alleged truth does not seem to be quite right. Ultimately, some may merely note a general degree of discomfort (since several independent models were presented) between a literal reading of the Bible and the current state of modern science. [16]

Notes:

[1] Science currently believes that in the beginning there was a extraordinary surge of energy that quickly "condensed" into a primordial gas (primarily hydrogen with a little helium). In addition to the two simplest elements, with atomic numbers one and two, there were also trace amounts of lithium and beryllium (the next elements on the periodic table with atomic numbers 3 and 4). In fairness, while there are many compelling reasons to believe this, there is no empirical evidence that completely pins this down yet.

[2] Most Biblical scholars place the temple around 966 BCE.

[3] Adam, first man, also based on 1 Cor.15:45 & 47

[4] It has been suggested that the creation days were not 24 hour type days. First, the Hebrew word yawm could be used to refer to long periods. Secondly, time is an unusual concept. This is noted in 2 Peter 3:8 and Psalm 90:4, where a day can be like a thousand years. This is a perfectly valid point and would easily allow for a more ancient creation under normal conditions. Unfortunately, there are three points that make it difficult for Christians to argue this point.

First, if the creation days are very long periods (e.g. 1000s of years, etc.) then between day and day the plants have been surviving without light for 1000s of years and thus would not be obeying normal scientific rules as we know them today.

Second, other Biblical verses explicitly qualify the creation days as normal days — not long periods. Specifically see:

Genesis 1:31: And the evening and the morning were the sixth day.

Exodus 20:8-11: Remember the Sabbath day, to keep it holy. Six days shalt thou labour, and do all thy work: But the seventh day is the sabbath of the Lord thy God: in it thou shalt not do any work, thou, nor thy son, nor thy daughter, thy manservant, nor thy maidservant, nor thy cattle, nor thy stranger that is within thy gates: For in six days the Lord made heaven and earth, the sea, and all that in them is, and rested the seventh day: wherefore the Lord blessed the sabbath day, and hallowed it.

31:14-17 Ye shall keep the sabbath therefore; for it is holy unto you: every one that defileth it shall surely be put to death: for whosoever doeth any work therein, that soul shall be cut off from among his people. Six days may work be done; but in the seventh is the sabbath of rest, holy to the Lord: whosoever doeth any work in the sabbath day, he shall surely be put to death. Wherefore the children of Israel shall keep the sabbath, to observe the sabbath throughout their generations, for a perpetual covenant. It is a sign between me and the children of Israel for ever: for in six days the Lord made heaven and earth, and on the seventh day he rested, and was refreshed.

(The counter argument presented for this has been

that the days represent "units of work" not actual 24 hour days.)

The third, perhaps more theologically thorny problem, is present is these verses:

Romans 5:12: Wherefore, as by one man sin entered into the world, and death by sin; and so death passed upon all men, for that all have sinned:

I Corith 15:21-22: For since by man came death, by man came also the resurrection of the dead. For as in Adam all die, even so in Christ shall all be made alive.

Was there death and affliction before Adam? How does this affect the notion of (physical) death arising because of sin? Was there death and affliction before Adam? It is difficult for death not to occur over thousands of years. (Science, based on consistent index fossil layering in the sedimentary strata suggests many species members died before the advent of man. Furthermore, the bracketing (in time) of these strata by intrusion of igneous dikes and presence of volcanic ash beds have allowed radiometric dating to establish upper and lower bounds of absolute dating for various strata. Individual strata have thus been shown to cover several thousand years. See brief discussion in the US Geological Survey article http:// pubs.usgs.gov/gip/geotime/contents.html). Thus there are many possible theological repercussions related to original sin, salvation, and the theory of atonement if one goes down this line of thought.

We should also ask about English translations of the meaning of the Quran which speak of six "days" of creation. (Note: There is no notion of God resting on the seventh day. Muslims reject the contradictory notion that an omnipotent being would require "rest.") It should be noted that the Arabic term yaum can also refer to long periods, so the translation could just as easily have read six periods instead of six days. Therefore this problem does not arise in the Quran. Some have tried to push this point with questionable hadith. But, questionable hadith – as any Muslim knows - do not form a foundation of Islam. If a particular hadith is proved unreliable, Islam still stands. There is indeed an entire Islamic science for separating authentic hadith from weak or unreliable ones. Therefore, this is not a problem for Muslims.

[5]Genesis 5:3 (Adam & Seth), 5:6 (Enos), 5:9(Cainan), 5:12 (Mahalaleel), 5:15 (Jared), 5:18 (Enoch), 5:21 (Methuselah), 5:25 (Lamech), 5:28-29 (Noah), 5:32;11:10;7:6(Shem), 11:10 (Arphaxad), 11:12 (Salah), 11:14 (Eber), 11:16 (Peleg), 11:18 (Reu), 11:20 (Serug), 11:22 (Nahor),11:24 (Terah), 11:26;11:32;12:4 (Abraham) . Note: There are no "gaps" in this reading.

[6] There are many ways to reach this number. Here is one quick approximation. I Kings 6:1 shows exodus about 480 years before the first temple (950 BCE – 480 BCE = 1430 BCE). Galatians 3: 17 shows Abraham's covenant with a gap of 430 years or 1860 BCE when Abraham was 75 (Genesis 12:1-4) putting Abraham's birth around 1935 BCE or around 20 centuries before Christ. (A more common method compiles the time of bondage and the ages of the patriarchs after establishing the date of the exodus from I King 6:1 and the building of the temple.)

[7] Note dating variations can occur since there are

several inconsistent Biblical texts and traditions. For example, in the Hebrew Pentateuch, creation is estimated at 4004 BCE but 5872 BCE in the Greek Septuagint, 4700 BCE Samaritan, and 4004 BCE for the well known Usher estimate.

[8] For more discussion try Ann Gibbons "Calibrating the Mitochondrial Clock." This area is currently unsettled, Different sources give substantially different estimates. Some estimates (using certain assumptions) can be substantially above 6,500 years. One should read the various sources (particularly the assumptions) carefully if one is interested in this area.

[9] Diversity of sample. Structural issues: Mitochondrial DNA (MtDNA) of women who don't have daughters won't be passing on MtDNA past their sons, and it will pass out of the MtDNA pool forever after the first generation. Sampling issues: Extreme example. If the only people left alive on the earth were you and your cousins, a sampling might not show any MtDNA variations resulting in time to a common ancestor of maybe eighty years (e.g., grandmother). Such a number is more useful as a lower bound rather than an absolute number to determine a "mitochondrial Eve" for humans in general. Assumptions about mutation rate. Is it constant? Short time "reversible"? etc.

[10] There is a male counterpart to "mitochondrial Eve" (or more precisely matrilineal most recent common ancestor). This male counterpart is called "Y-chromosome Adam" (or more precisely patrilineal human most recent common ancestor).

Y-chromosomes that are transmitted in a direct line from father to son are largely unchanged except for random mutations over time. For example, if a specific rate of change is assumed, the changes can be rolled back to date the oldest father in such a line based on certain assumptions. Using a similar techniques to those discussed and certain assumptions, geneticist Spencer Wells has dated the oldest father in such a transmission line, and based on a certain population sample, to a certain number of years.

There are several methods that have been used to date humans. Currently, there are scientists that believe that modern humans have been around for at least 100,000 years. The actual timescale among many different scientists may depend on what evidence and methods they accord greater weight to and to evidence and techniques that will be uncovered in the future.

Some similiar to the theories discussed by population geneticists and molecular biologists may look at things like genes (DNA/MtDNA, etc.) While examining DNA/MtDNA they may use concepts   like genetic drift and/or Monte Carlo simulations/combinatorial/ statistical arguments. Others like archaeologists, paleoanthropologists and paleoclimatologists may take a greater interest in our environment (for example, fossil record, isotopes in ice cores). Furthermore, the assumptions used in each model, could dramatically impact projected results. So all assumptions (particularly hidden, implicit ones) should be carefully analyzed. These results may not all agree precisely, and may themselves be subject to revision. In conclusion, this area appears to be in some flux.

[11] Widespread use of the terms "Mitochondrial Eve" and "Y-chromosomal Adam" is unfortunate. The discussed techniques of mitrochondiral DNA and y-chromosome analysis do not "prove" the existence

of a scriptural "Adam" and "Eve." For example, it is possible for opponents to suggest that other females lived at the time of "mitrochondrial Eve" but that they were wiped out in catastrophic event and "Eve" survived. There are however different theories that talk about the lack of genetic diversity in humans compared to other species and suggest possible population bottlenecks.

[12] Wise (1998a:171)

[13] Actually an even more robust technique was used to estimate the age of the solar system. Three lead isotopes (Pb-208, Pb-207, Pb-204) are used in isochrone (see http://www.talkorigins.org   faqs on isochrone dating) dating with samples of earth and meteorites.   See www.talkorigins.org faq on age of earth for this as well as for some Ar-Ar, Rb-Sr, Sm-Nd meteorite examples.

[14] See "Age of Universe" at the nasa website. http://map.gsfc.nasa.gov/universe/uni_age.html

[15] In contrast, the Quranic account which is not so emphatic about the flood being global, unlike the Biblical account, easily allows for the possible interpretation of a local flood, sent only against the evildoers where Noah was resident.   Likewise, the animals on the ark can easily be interpreted as a stop gap sustenance measure for the period of the local flood and a short time afterwards, not as an attempt to preserve the entire world's species.

[16] It is not our intention to malign anyone for emotional reasons, we merely present "food for thought" and ultimately a meritocracy of ideas may prevail. We ourselves remain open to updating this section or even eliminating it.

Chapter 13

Quran Preserved?

By Sabeel Ahmed

Perhaps unlike any other religion, Islam has zealously guarded and protected its original relevation over hundreds of years from human encroachment, embellishments and interpolations. Muslims believe this is necessary to prevent a tide of man-made amendments from overwhelming divine dictates (either intentionally or unintentionally) and thus usurping divine right and decree.

Imagine this scenario: A professor gives a three hour lecture to his students. Imagine still that none of the students memorized this speech of the professor or wrote it down. Now forty years after that speech, if these same students decided to replicate the professor's complete speech word for word, would they be able to do it? Obviously not, because the only two modes of preservation historically is through writing and memory. If the memorization part doesn't exist parallel to the written part to act as a check and balance for it, then there is a genuine possibility that the written scripture might loose its purity through unintentional and/or intentional interpolations due to scribal errors, corruption by the enemies, pages decomposing etc, these errors would be concurrently incorporated into subsequent texts, so that the original would ultimately lose its purity through the ages.

It should be noted that few religions possess their revelations both in writing and in memory from the day of their original revelations until our time. However, this is one of the salient characteristics of Islam and the Muslim holy book, the Quran. Muslims will note that the Quran has been zealously protected both in writing and memory for hundreds of years.

TRANSMISSION OF THE QUR'AN: ORAL & WRITTEN

Let us analyze the claim of the Quran's preservation.

1. MEMORIZATION

Earlier in human history, before writing became widespread, "memory and oral transmission were exercised and strengthened to a degree now almost unknown" relates Michael Zwettler.[1]

Prophet Muhammad, The First Memorizer
It was in this "oral" society that Prophet Muhammad was born in Mecca in the year 570 C.E. At the age of 40, he started receiving divine revelations from Allah through Archangel Gabriel. This process of divine revelations continued for about 22.5 years until just before he passed away.

Prophet Muhammad memorized each revelation and

used to proclaim it to his companions. Angel Gabriel used to refresh the Quranic memory of the Prophet each year.

According to Sahih Bukhari 6.15a,
"The Prophet was the most generous person, and he used to become more so (generous) particularly in the month of Ramadan because Gabriel used to meet him every night of the month of Ramadan until it ended. Allah's Messenger used to recite the Qur'an for Gabriel. When Gabriel met him, he used to become more generous than the fast wind in doing good." [2]

"Gabriel used to repeat the recitation of the Qur'an with the Prophet once a year, but he repeated it twice with him in the year he (the Prophet) died." [3]

The Prophet himself used to stay up a greater part of the night in prayers and use to recite the Quran from memory.

PROPHET'S COMPANIONS: THE FIRST GENERATION MEMORIZERS

Prophet Muhammad (S) encouraged his companions to learn and teach the Quran:

"The most superior among you (Muslims) are those who learn the Qur'an and teach it." [4]

"Some of the companions who memorized the Quran were: 'Abu Bakr, Umar, Uthman, Ali, Ibn Masud, Abu Huraira, Abdullah bin Abbas, Abdullah bin Amr bin al-As, Aisha, Hafsa, and Umm Salama'." [5]

"Abu Bakr, the first male Muslim to convert to Islam used to recite the Quran publicly in front of his house in Makka." [6]

The Prophet also listened to the recitation of the Qur'an by the companions: "Allah's Apostle said to me (Abdullah bin Mas'ud): 'Recite (of the Quran) to me,' I said: 'Shall I recite it to you although it had been revealed to you?!' He said: 'I like to hear (the Quran) from others.' So I recited Sura-an-Nisa' until I reached: 'How (will it be) then when We bring from each nation a witness and We bring you (O Muhammad) as a witness against these people?' (4:41) Then he said: 'Stop!' Behold, his eyes then were shedding tears.'" [7]

Many Quranic memorizers (Qurra) were present during the lifetime of the Prophet and afterwards throughout the then Muslim world.

At the battle of Yamama, many memorizers of the Quran were martyred. "Narrated Zaid bin Thabit al Ansari, who was one of those who use to write the divine revelations: Abu Bakr sent me after the (heavy) casualties among the warriors (of the battle) of Yamama (where a great number of Qurra were killed). Umar was present with Abu Bakr who said: 'Umar has come to me and said, "the people have suffered heavy casualties on the day of (the battle of) Yamama, and I am afraid that there will be some casualties among the Qurra (those who memorized the entire Quran) at other places...'"." [8]

"Thousands of schools devoted specially to the

teaching of the Quran to children for the purpose of memorization" have flourished through the ages during Muslim history. Caliph Umar (634-44), it is claimed, ordered school construction during a period of great expansion. [9]

SECOND GENERATION MEMORIZERS

"...Quranic schools were set up everywhere. As an example to illustrate this, I may refer to a great Muslim scholar of the second Muslim generation, Ibn 'Amir, who was the judge of Damascus under the Caliph Umar Ibn 'Abd Al-Aziz. It is reported that in his school for teaching the Quran there were 400 disciples to teach in his absence." [10]

MEMORIZERS IN SUBSEQUENT GENERATIONS

Estimates exist of over two thousand such schools (in Arabic: Katatib) in Cairo (Egypt) alone, at one time. [11]

Currently both in the Muslim and non-Muslim countries there are thousands of schools with each instructing tens of hundreds of students in the art of memorizing the entire Quran. In the city of Chicago itself, there are close to 40 mosques, with many of them holding class for children to instruct them in the art of Quranic memorization.

FURTHER POINTS OF CONSIDERATION

Muslims recite the Quran from memory in all of their five daily prayers. Once a year during the month of Fasting (Ramadan), Muslims listen to the complete recitation of the Quran by a Hafiz (memorizer of the entire Quran). It is a tradition among Muslims that before any speech or presentation, marriages, or sermons, the Quran is recited.

CONCLUSION

The Quran is the only book, religious or secular, on the face of this planet that has been completely memorized by millions. These memorizers range from age 6 and up, both Arabic and non-Arabic speakers, blacks, whites, Orientals, poor and wealthy. Thus the process of memorization was continuous, from the time of Prophet Muhammad to ours with an unbroken chain.

The use of memorization in oral transmission through the generations "had mitigated somewhat from the beginning the worst perils of relying solely on written records," relates John Burton. [12]

The tradition of an oral transmission through the centuries in "unbroken living sequence of devotion." reflects Kenneth Craig, helps render it as a instrument of the present not a historical artifact. [13]

2. WRITTEN TEXT OF THE QURAN

Prophet's Lifetime:
Prophet Muhammad was very vigilant in preserving the Quran in written form from the very beginning up until the last revelation. The Prophet himself was unlettered, did not knew how to read and write, and therefore he called upon his numerous scribes to write the revelation for him. The complete Quran thus existed in written form in the lifetime of the

Prophet.

Whenever a new revelation used to come to him, the Prophet would immediately call one of his scribes to write it down.

"Some people visited Zaid Ibn Thabit (one of the scribes of the Prophet) and asked him to tell them some stories about Allah's Messenger. He replied, 'I was his (Prophet's) neighbor, and when the inspiration descended on him he sent for me and I went to him and wrote it down for him'." [14]

Narrated al-Bara': "There was revealed 'Not equal are those believers who sit (home) and those who strive and fight in the cause of Allah' (4:95). The Prophet said: 'Call Zaid for me and let him bring the board, the ink pot, and scapula bone.' Then he (Prophet) said: 'Write: Not equal are those believers ...' "[15]

Zaid is reported to have said: "We used to compile the Qur'an from small scraps in the presence of the Apostle." [16]

"The Prophet, while in Madinah, had about 48 scribes who used to write for him." [17]

Abdullah Ibn 'Umar relates: "The Messenger of Allah said: 'Do not take the Qur'an on a journey with you, for I am afraid that it might fall into the hands of the enemy'." [18]

During the Prophet's last pilgrimage, he gave a sermon in which he said: "I have left with you something with which, if you will hold fast to it, you will never fall into error - a plain indication, the Book of God (Quran) and the practice of his Prophet." [19]

"Besides the official manuscripts of the Quran kept with the Prophet, many of his companions used to possess their own written copies of the revelation." [20]

"A list of companions of whom it is related that they had their own written collections included the following: Ibn Mas'ud, Ubay bin Ka'b, Ali, Ibn Abbas, Abu Musa, Hafsa, Anas bin Malik, Umar, Zaid bin Thabit, Ibn Al-Zubair, Abdullah ibn Amr, Aisha, Salim, Umm Salama, Ubaid bin Umar." [21]

"The best known among these (the Prophet's scribes) are Ibn Masud, Ubay bin Kab and Zaid bin Thabit." [22]

"Aisha and Hafsa, the wives of the Prophet had their own scripts written after the Prophet had died." [23]

CONCLUSION

The complete Quran was written down in front of the Prophet by several of his scribes, and the companions possessed their own copies of the Quran in the Prophet's lifetime. The written material of the Quran in the Prophet's possession, however, was not bound between two covers in the form of a book, because the period of revelation of the Qur'an continued up until just a few days before the Prophet's death. The task of collecting the Qur'an as a book was therefore undertaken by Abu Bakr, the first successor to the Prophet.

WRITTEN QUR'AN IN FIRST GENERATION

At the battle of Yamama (633 CE), six months after the death of the Prophet, a number of Muslims who had memorized the Quran were killed. Hence it was feared that unless an official written copy of the Quran was prepared, a large part of revelation might be lost.

Narrated Zaid bin Thabit al-Ansari, one of the scribes of the revelation," Abu Bakr sent for me after the casualties among the warriors (of the battle) of Yamama, where a great number of Qurra (memorizers of the Quran) were killed. Umar was present with Abu Bakr who said, 'Umar has come to me and said, the people have suffered heavy casualties on the day of (the battle) of Yamama, and I am afraid that there will be some casualties among the Qurra at other places, whereby a large part of the Quran may be lost, unless you collect it (in one manuscript, or book) ... so Abu Bakr said to me (Zaid bin Thabit), "You are a wise young man and we do not suspect you (of telling lies or of forgetfulness), and you used to write the Divine Inspiration for Allah's Apostle. Therefore, look for the Qur'an and collect it (in one manuscript)"...'So I started locating the Quranic material and collecting it from parchments, scapula, leafstalks of date palms and from the memories of men (who know it by heart) '." [24]

Now, a committee was formed to undertake the task of collecting the written Quranic material in the form of a book. The committee was headed by Zaid bin Thabit, the original scribe of the Prophet, who was also a memorizer of the complete Quran.

One of those who had memorized the entire Quran was Zaid bin Thabit. [25]

The compilers in this committee, in examining written material submitted to them, insisted on very stringent criteria as a safeguard against any errors.

1) The material must have been originally written down in the presence of the Prophet; nothing written down later on the basis of memory alone was to be accepted. [26]

2) The material must be confirmed by two witnesses, that is to say, by two trustworthy persons testifying that they themselves had heard the Prophet recite the passage in question. [27]

"The manuscript on which the Qur'an was collected, remained with Abu Bakr until Allah took him unto Himself, and then with Umar (the second successor), until Allah took him, and finally it remained with Hafsa, 'Umar's daughter (and wife of the Prophet)." [28]

This copy of the Quran, prepared by the committee of competent companions of the Prophet (which included memorizers of the Quran), was unanimously approved by the whole Muslim world. If the committee would have made an error even of a single letter in transcribing the Quran, the Qurra (memorizers of the Quran), which totaled in the tens of hundreds, would have caught it right away and corrected it. This is exactly where the neat check and balance system of preservation of the Quran comes into play, but which is lacking for any other scripture besides the Quran.

OFFICIAL WRITTEN COPY BY UTHMAN

The Quran was originally revealed in the Quraishi dialect of Arabic. But to facilitate the understanding and comprehension of the people who speak other dialects, the Quran was memorized in seven dialects of Arabic. During the period of Caliph Uthman (second successor to the Prophet) differences in reading the Quran among the various tribes became obvious, due to the various dialectical recitations. Dispute was arising, with each tribe calling its recitation the correct one. This alarmed Uthman, who made an official copy in the Quraishi dialect, the dialect in which the Quran was first revealed to the Prophet and was memorized by his companions. Thus this compilation by Uthman's committee was not a different version of the Quran (like the Biblical versions) but the same original revelation given to the Prophet by the One God, Allah.

Narrated Anas bin Malik: "Hudhaifa bin Al-Yaman came to Uthman at the time when the people of Sham (Syria) and the people of Iraq were waging war to conquer Armenia and Azherbijan. Hudhaifa was afraid of their differences in the recitation of the Quran, so he said to Uthman, 'O chief of the Believers! Save this nation before they differ about the Book (Quran) as Jews and Christians did before,' So Uthman sent a message to Hafsa saying, 'Send us the manuscripts of the Quran so that we may compile the Quranic materials in perfect copies and return the manuscripts to you,' Hafsa sent it to Uthman.

'Uthman then ordered Zaid bin Thabit, 'Abdullah bin Az-Zubair, Said bin Al-As, and Abdur Rahman bin Harith bin Hisham to rewrite the manuscripts in perfect copies. Uthman said to the three Quraishi men, 'In case you disagree with Zaid bin Thabit on any point in the Quran, then write it in their (Quraishi) tongue.' They did so, and when they had written many copies, Uthman sent to every Muslim province one copy of what they had copied and ordered that all the other Quranic materials whether written in fragmentary manuscripts or whole copies, be burned..." [29]

Again very stringent criteria were set up by this committee to prevent any alteration of the revelation.

1) The earlier recension (original copy prepared by Abu Bakr) was to serve as the principal basis of the new one. [30]

2) Any doubt that might be raised as to the phrasing of a particular passage in the written text was to be dispelled by summoning persons known to have learned the passage in question from the Prophet. [31]

3) Uthman himself was to supervise the work of the Council. [32]

When the final recension was completed, Uthman sent a copy of it to each of the major cities of Makka, Damascus, Kufa, Basra, and Madina.

The action of Uthman to burn all copies other than

the final recension, though obviously drastic, was for the betterment and harmony of the whole community and was unanimously approved by the companions of the Prophet.

Zaid ibn Thabit is reported to have said: "I saw the Companions of Muhammad (going about) saying, 'By God, Uthman has done well! By God, Uthman has done well!" [33]

Another esteemed companion, Musab ibn Sad ibn Abi Waqqas, said: "I saw the people assemble in large number at Uthman's burning of the proscribed copies (of the Quran), and they were all pleased with his action; not a one spoke out against him." [34]

Ali ibn Abu Talib, the cousin of the Prophet and the fourth successor to the Prophet commented: "If I were in command in place of Uthman, I would have done the same." [35]

Of the copies made by Uthman, two still exist to our day. One is in the city of Tashkent (Uzbekistan), and the second one is in Istanbul (Turkey). Below is a brief account of both these copies:

The copy which Uthman sent to Madina was reportedly removed by the Turkish authorities to Istanbul, from where it came to Berlin during World War I. The Treaty of Versailles, which concluded World War I, contains the following clause:

"Article 246: Within six months from the coming into force of the present Treaty, Germany will restore to His Majesty, King of Hedjaz, the original Koran of

Caliph Othman, which was removed from Madina by the Turkish authorities and is stated to have been presented to the ex-Emperor William II." [36]

"This manuscript then reached Istanbul (where it now resides), but not Madina ." [37]

The second copy in existence is kept in Tashkent, Uzbekistan. "It may be the Imam (master) manuscript or one of the other copies made at the time of Uthman." [38]

It came to Samarkand in 890 Hijra (1485) and remained there till 1868. Then it was taken to St. Petersburg by the Russians in 1869. It remained there until 1917. A Russian orientalist gave a detailed description of it, saying that many pages were damaged and some were missing. A facsimile in some 50 copies of this mushaf (copy) was produced by S. Pisareff in 1905. A copy was sent to the Ottoman Sultan 'Abdul Hamid, to the Shah of Iran, to the Amir of Bukhara, to Afghanistan, to Fas and some important Muslim personalities. One copy is now in the Columbia University Library (U.S.A.). [39]

"The manuscript was afterwards returned to its former place and reached Tashkent in 1924, where it has remained since." [40]

CONCLUSION

"Two of the copies of the Qur'an that were originally prepared in the time of Caliph Uthman are still available to us today and their text and arrangement can be compared by anyone who cares to do so with any other copy of the Quran, be it in print or handwritten, from any place or period of time. They will be found [to be] identical." [41]

It can now be proclaimed through the evidence provided above, with full conviction and certainty, that the Prophet memorized the entire Quran and had it written down in front of him by his scribes; many of his companions memorized the entire revelation and in turn possessed their own private copies for recitation and contemplation. This process of dual preservation of the Quran in writing and in the memory was carried down in each subsequent generation until our time, without any deletion, interpolation, or corruption.

Sir William Muir states, "There is probably in the world no other book which has remained twelve centuries [now fourteen] with so pure a text." [42]

Additionally, another Christian missionary makes this profound, yet true statement: "What we have today in our hands is the Mushaf of Muhammad." [43]

This divine protection provided to the Quran, is proclaimed by God in the Quran:

"[Allah] has, without doubt, sent down the Message; and will assuredly Guard it (from corruption)" (Quran - chapter 15, verse 9).

Compare this divine and historical preservation of the Quran with any literature, be it religious or secular, and it becomes evident that none possesses similar provenance. As stated earlier, a belief is as authentic as the authenticity of its scripture. If any scripture is not preserved, how can we be certain that the belief arising out of this scripture is divine or man made?

Thus, the above evidence for the protection of the Quran from any corruption is a strong hint about its divine origin.

NOTES

1. Michael Zwettler, *The Oral Tradition of Classical Arabic Poetry*, p.14. Ohio State Press: 1978.

2. Transmitted by Ibn Abbas, collected in *Sahih Al-Bukhari, 6.519*, translated by Dr. Muhammad Muhsin Khan.

3. Transmitted by Abu Hurayrah, collected in *Sahih Al-Bukhari, 6.520*, translated by Dr. Muhammad Muhsin Khan.

4. Transmitted by Uthman bin Affan, collected in *Sahih Bukhari, 6.546*, translated by Dr. Muhammad Muhsin Khan.

5. Jalal al-Din Suyuti, *Al-Itqan fi-ulum al-Quran*, vol. I, p. 124.

6. Ibn Hisham, *Sira al-Nabi*, Cairo, n.d., Vol.I, p. 206.

7. Al-Bukhari, 6.106.

8. Al-Bukhari, 6.201.

9. Labib as-Said, *The Recited Koran*, tr. Bernard Weiss, M. A. Rauf, and Morroe Berger, The Darwin Press, Princeton, New Jersey, 1975, pg. 58.

10. Ibn al Jazari, *Kitab al-Nash fi al-Qir'at al-Ashr*, Cairo, Al-Halabi, n.d. vol. 2, p. 254; also Ahmad Makki al-Ansari, *Al-Difa' 'An al-Qur'an*. Cairo, Dar al-Ma'arif, 1973 C.E., part I, p. 120.

11. Labib as-Said, *The Recited Koran*, tr. Bernard Weiss, M. A. Rauf, and Morroe Berger, The Darwin Press, Princeton, New Jersey, 1975, pg. 59.

12. John Burton, *An Introduction to the Hadith*, Edinburgh University Press: 1994, p. 27.

13. Kenneth Cragg, *The Mind of the Qur'an*, George Allen & Unwin: 1973, p.26.

14. Tirmidhi, *Mishkat al-Masabih*, no. 5823.

15. *Al-Bukhari*, 6.512.

16. Suyuti, *Itqan, I*, p. 99.

17. M. M. Azami, *Kuttab al-Nabi*, Beirut, 1974.

18. *Muslim*, III, no. 4606; also 4607, 4608; Bukhari, 4.233.

19. Ibn Hisham, *Sira al-Nabi*, p. 651.

20. Suyuti, *Itqan, I*, p. 62.

21. Ibn Abi Dawud, *Masahif*, p. 14.

22. Bayard Dodge, *The fihrist of al-Nadim: A Tenth Century Survey of Muslim Culture*, New York, 1970, pp. 53-63.

23. Imam Malik, *Muwatta*, tr. M. Rahimuddin, Lahore, 1980, no.307, 308.

24. *Bukhari*, 6.201.

25. Labib as-Said, *The Recited Koran*, tr. Bernard Weiss, et al., 1975, p. 21.

26. Ibn Hajar, *Fath*, Vol. IX, p. 10.

27. ibid., p. 11.

28. *Bukhari*, 6.201.

29. *Bukhari*, 6.510.

30. Ibn Hajar, *Bath*, IX, p. 15.

31. Suyuti, *Itqan*, Vol.I, p. 59.

32. ibid., p. 59.

33. Naysaburi, al-Nizam al-Din al-Hasan ibn Muhammad, *Ghara'ib al-Quran wa-Ragha'ib al-furqan*, 4 vols., to date. Cairo, 1962.

34. Ibn Abi Dawud, p. 12.

35. Zarkashi, al-Badr al-Din, *Al-Burhan fi-Ulum al-Quran*, Cairo, 1957, vol. I, p. 240.

36. Fred L. Israel, *Major Peace Treaties of Modern History*, New York, Chelsea House Pub., Vol. II, p. 1418.

37. Makhdum, op. cit., 1938, p. 19.

38. Ahmad von Denffer, *Ulum Al-Qur'an*, revised ed., Islamic Foundation, 1994, p. 63.

39. *The Muslim World*, vol. 30 (1940), pp. 357-8.

40. Ahmad von Denffer, *Ulum Al-Quran*, revised ed., Islamic Foundation, 1994, p. 63.

41. ibid., p. 64.

42. Sir Williams Muir, *Life of Mohamet*, vol.1, Introduction.

43. John Burton, *The Collection Of the Quran*, 1977, Cambridge University Press, pp. 239-240.

15

Jesus: Man and God?

By Jerald F. Dirks, M.Div., Psy.D.

INTRODUCTION

That Jesus is both God and man simultaneously is directly stated in the so-called Nicene Creed issued by the Council of Constantinople in 381 and in the creedal formulation issued by the Council of Ephesus in 431. The simultaneous god-man dichotomy finds its fullest expression, however, in the statement issued by the Council of Chalcedon in 451:

> "...our Lord Jesus Christ, perfect in deity and perfect in humanity... in two natures, without being mixed, transmuted, divided, or separated. The distinction between the natures is by no means done away with through the union, but rather the identity of each nature is preserved and concurs into one person and being. "

There are two natures that are neither "mixed" nor "separated," yet "the distinction between" the human and divine "is preserved." How are two things distinct from each other, yet not separated or divided? To use the analogy of apples and oranges, an apple is distinct from an orange, just as the alleged divinity of Jesus is said to be distinct from his humanity. But, that very distinction makes it logically impossible that the apple and the orange are not "divided or separated" from each other. Furthermore, one cannot resolve this dilemma by dropping the apple and the orange into a blender and pureeing them, because the doctrine tells us that the two natures are not "mixed, transmuted" or "done away with through the union." Clearly, this is a doctrine that can be maintained only through recourse to the phrase "divine mystery," because it defies all human reason, logic, and intellect.

It is perhaps because the doctrine of Jesus as both God and man is so difficult to comprehend that one finds a variety of beliefs about the nature of Jesus among Christians, despite the "official" statement of the Council of Chalcedon. In a nutshell, these beliefs can be categorized into three different positions: 1) Jesus is God; 2) Jesus is both God and man simultaneously; and 3) Jesus was a man, although one who was divinely inspired by God. Common to the first two positions is the belief that Jesus was divine in some way or other. In what follows, all three positions are addressed, although the first two are discussed jointly, as they both allege the divinity of Jesus.

JESUS VS. GOD

The *Bible* gives several examples in which Jesus distinguishes himself as being separate from God and clearly subordinates himself to God.

But of that day and that hour knoweth no man, no, not the angels which are in heaven, neither the Son, but the Father (*Mark* 13:32).

And Jesus said unto him, Why callest thou me good? There is none good but one, that is, God. (*Mark* 10:18; see also *Matthew* 19:17 and *Luke* 18:19).

Then answered Jesus and said unto them, Verily, verily, I say unto you, The Son can do nothing of himself, but what he seeth the Father do: for what things soever he doeth, these also doeth the Son likewise...I can of mine own self do nothing: as I hear, I judge: and my judgment is just: because I seek not mine own will, but the will of the Father which hath sent me (*John* 5:19, 30)

... my Father is greater than I (*John* 14:28).

...I ascend unto my Father and your Father; and to my God, and your God (*John* 20:17).

Of these verses, the last is particularly striking, for Jesus reportedly said that he was going "to my God, and your God," which appears to be an explicit denial of his being God. There is one more verse that needs to be presented, one which says that after his ascension Jesus "sat down at the right hand of God," obviously implying that Jesus and God are separate and distinct entities.

So then after the Lord had spoken unto them, he was received up into heaven, and sat on the right hand of God (*Mark* 16:19).

Of most importance in considering this last verse, one should note that the verse does not say that Jesus sat down at the right hand of "the Father," but that he "sat on the right hand of God." As such, attempts to salvage a Jesus-as-God concept from this verse cannot resort to contrasting "the Son" with "the Father," but are forced to contrast Jesus with God.

Additional Biblical examples of the separation of Jesus from God are readily available: 1) *James* 1:13 says that God cannot be tempted, yet *Matthew* 4:1-11, *Mark* 1:12-13, and *Luke* 4:1-15 say that Jesus was tempted; 2) *I Kings* 8:27 states that God cannot dwell on earth or be contained, yet Jesus dwelt on earth. Further, how did the body of Jesus contain the uncontainable? 3) The *Bible* repeatedly says that Jesus prayed to God and asked things of Him (*Matthew* 14:23, 19:13, 26:39-44, 27:46; *Mark* 1:35, 6:45-46, 14:35-36, 15:33-34; *Luke* 3:21, 5:16, 6:12, 9:18 & 28, 11:1, 22:41-44, 23:46; *John* 14:16, 17:1-15), implying Jesus's separation from and subordination to God; 4) God is all-powerful, yet Jesus needed to be strengthened by an angel (*Luke* 22:43); 5) Speaking out against Jesus can be forgiven, but speaking out against the Holy Ghost will never be forgiven (*Matthew* 12:32).

Finally, the *Bible* has Jesus frequently referring to himself as the "son of man" (e.g., *Matthew* 8:20, 9:6, 10:23, 11:19, 12:8 & 12:32, 13:37-41, 16:13 & 27-28, 17:22; 24:27-31, 26:24, 45, & 64). But, the *Bible* also states that God is not a man or the son of man.

God is not a man, that he should lie; neither the son of man, that he should repent (*Numbers* 23:19).

THE "SON OF GOD"

Some Christians may want to cling to the alleged divinity of Jesus by reference to the concept of the "Son of God" as stated in *Matthew* 16:16. However, a quick perusal of the *Bible* demonstrates that "Son of God" was a title that was used metaphorically, not literally. For example, the *Bible* refers to all of the following individuals and groups as being the "Son of God": 1) the people of Israel (*Exodus* 4:22; *Hosea* 11:1-3; and *Jeremiah* 31:9); 2) the Israelite sub-tribe of Ephraim (*Jeremiah* 31:9, 20); 3) David (*Psalms* 2:7 and 89:3, 26-27); 4) Solomon (*II Samuel* 7:13-14—it was Solomon who built the "house"/temple of God in Jerusalem); 5) the angels (*Job* 1:6); and 6) all faithful Israelites (*Deuteronomy* 14:1). As can be seen by these above verses, the *Bible* refers to numerous people and entities as being the "Son of God."

JESUS AS PROPHET

Islam and the *Qur'an* view Jesus as being a man, although a man who was a prophet and messenger of God. The *Bible* provides numerous references indicating that the contemporaries of Jesus also viewed him as being a prophet, not a deity. A representative sampling of these references includes *Matthew* 21:10-11, 45-46; *Mark* 6:14-15; *Luke* 7:14-16, 9:7-8, 24:19; and *John* 4:16-19, 6:14, 7:40, 9:17. As these verses demonstrate, the contemporaries of Jesus Christ repeatedly considered him to be a prophet. It mattered not whether those contemporaries were the crowds of Jerusalem, the Israelite people in general, those who had witnessed the reported miracles of Jesus, those who had talked with Jesus and been confronted by him, or those who were healed by him. Across all these groups, the above verses of the *New Testament* indicate that there was a consensus that Jesus was a prophet of one kind or another.

Having presented the above, it must be acknowledged that the Christian reader will probably be quick to claim that these contemporaries of Jesus were wrong and that they misperceived him and did not know him well enough to understand him and his "divine" nature. It is instructive to note, however, that neither Jesus nor the authors of the *New Testament* books cited above ever said that the contemporaries of Jesus were wrong in saying that he was a prophet. Moreover, in several *New Testament* passages, Jesus appears to be referring to himself as being a prophet.

> He that receiveth you receiveth me, and he that receiveth me receiveth him that sent me. He that receiveth a prophet in the name of a prophet shall receive a prophet's reward; and he that receiveth a righteous man in the name of a righteous man shall receive a righteous man's reward. (*Matthew* 10:40-41)

Several points need to be made with regard to the above quoted verses: 1) The statement that "he that receiveth me receiveth him that sent me" cannot be used to equate the nature of Jesus with that of God unless one is willing to use the statement that "he that receiveth you receiveth me" equates the nature of others with that of Jesus, and then by extension with that of God; 2) The first sentence also has Jesus referring to "him that sent me," clearly implying that Jesus was subordinate to the One who sent him; 3) If the statement that "(h)e that receiveth a prophet" is not a self-reference to Jesus' own prophethood, then to what prophet is Jesus referring? This becomes a crucial question, because the alleged statement of Jesus is not made in the past tense.

In a second statement attributed to Jesus, he refers to himself and to his having just been rejected by the people of Nazareth after attempting to preach there.

> But Jesus said unto them, A prophet is not without honour save in his own country, and in his own house. (*Matthew* 13:57; see also *Mark* 6:1-4, *Luke* 4:16-24, and *John* 4:43-44.)

In a third statement attributed to Jesus, albeit one that is sometimes interpreted by Christians as referring to the alleged crucifixion of Jesus, Jesus again refers to himself as being a prophet.

> Nevertheless I must walk today and tomorrow, and the day following: for it cannot be that a prophet perish out of Jerusalem. (*Luke* 13:33).

JESUS AND ADOPTIONISM

Given the above Biblical verses, how is one to understand the title of "Son of God" when it is applied to Jesus? The answer is to be found in the Adoptionist movement within early Christianity. The Adoptionist trajectory in early Christianity begins with the baptism of Jesus by John the Baptist. According to the usual Adoptionist formulations, it was at his moment of baptism that Jesus moved into his special relationship or metaphorical "sonship" with God—not at his conception or virgin birth. With regard to the baptism of Jesus, the account of *Luke* is especially relevant. As noted in appropriate footnotes to the Revised Standard Version and the New Revised Standard Version of the *Bible*, the oldest Greek manuscripts of and quotations from *Luke* render the key verse in question as follows.

Now when all the people were baptized, and when Jesus also had been baptized and was praying, the heaven was opened, and the Holy Spirit descended upon him in bodily form like a dove. And a voice came from heaven, "You are my son; today I have begotten you" (*Luke* 3:21-22).

"Today I have begotten you," i.e., at the time of baptism, not at the time of conception. Given that Jesus was clearly an adult at the time of his baptism, under this ancient reading of *Luke*, "begotten" must be understood metaphorically, not physically or literally. In other words, the "sonship" of Jesus was a created relationship, not a begotten relationship. Furthermore, before the contemporary Christian rejects this most ancient wording of *Luke* 3:22, he should realize that this exact wording regarding the baptism of Jesus is also to be found in *Hebrews* 1:5a, *Hebrews* 5:5, and *Acts* 13:33. This same wording is also found in *Psalms* 2:7 in reference to David and in the apocryphal *Gospel of the Ebionites* in reference to the baptism of Jesus.

THE EARLY CHURCH AND ADOPTIONISM

Numerous examples of Adoptionism and of the subordination of Jesus to God can be found within the history of the early church, e.g., the Ebionites, the Elkesaites, the Nazarenes (not to be confused with the modern denomination of the same name), Theodotianism or Dynamic Monarchianism, Arianism, Anomoeism, Nestorianism, and the Paulicians of Armenia. Furthermore, a listing of key individuals who supported an Adoptionist position or the subordination of Jesus to God reads like a *Who's Who* of early Christianity. Included among these individuals are: 1) Theodotus the Tanner, a second-century theologian; 2) Origen, a third-century priest, theologian, and head of the catechetical school at Alexandria; 3) Dionysius, a third-century bishop and head of the catechetical school at Alexandria; 4) Paul of Samosata, a third-century bishop of Antioch; 5) St. Lucian of Antioch, a third-century theologian; 6) Arius, a fourth-century priest at Alexandria; 7) Eusebius of Nicomedia, a fourth-century bishop of Berytus and Nicomedia; 8) Macedonius, a fourth-century bishop and patriarch of Constantinople; 9) Aetius, a fourth-century deacon at Antioch, who was later elevated to the episcopacy in 361; 10) Nestorius, a fifth-century bishop and patriarch of Constantinople; 11) Theodore of Mopsuestia, a fifth-century "guardian of right faith" in the Persian church; and 12) St. Clothilda, a fifth and sixth-century princess of Burgundy and queen of the Salian Franks.

While space does not permit a review of each of the above, it is instructive to look at the teachings of Arius. Arius taught that God is absolutely unique and incomparable, is alone self-existent, unchangeable, and infinite, and must be understood in terms of his absolute Oneness. Given this all-important first premise, Arius concluded that: 1) the life of Jesus demonstrates that Jesus was not self-existent, that he changed and grew over time, if in no other way than in passing through the stages of birth, childhood, adolescence, and adulthood, and that he was finite, having a definite time of conception and birth; 2) therefore Jesus was God's created being, who was called into existence out of nothingness, who could not have shared in the absolute uniqueness, immutability, and infinity of the Godhead without compromising them, who could not have been of the same substance as God without compromising the Oneness of God, and who could have had no direct knowledge of God, other than that which God chose to reveal to him.

Many Christians mistakenly believe that the questions concerning the nature of Jesus were resolved at the Council of Nicaea in 325 with the issuance of a doctrine saying that Jesus and God were of the same substance or essence. But a quick review of the decisions of subsequent church councils reveals that the issue was hardly resolved. For example, the Council of Antioch in 341 released a new creed that omitted any mention of Jesus and God being of one substance. Furthermore, at the Council of Sirmium in 357, the creedal formulation was that Jesus was unlike God. Only in 381, at the Council of Constantinople, was the Adoptionist position temporarily put to rest by the issuance of the so-called Nicene Creed. But, Adoptionism was so popular, probably representing the majority position within

Christianity through at least the fourth century, that repeated church councils had to reaffirm the Nicene Christology.

JESUS IN ISLAM

Like many Adoptionists among the early Christian saints, theologians, and bishops, Islam maintains that Jesus was a man, albeit one who was a prophet and messenger of God and who performed many miracles by God's leave. Islam also affirms the virgin birth of Jesus, but sees this as a miraculous creation, not as an act of divine begetting.

> Behold! the angels said: "O Mary! Allah hath chosen thee and purified thee—chosen thee above the women of all nations... Behold! the angels said: "O Mary! Allah giveth thee glad tidings of a word from Him: his name will be Christ Jesus. The son of Mary, held in honour in this world and the hereafter and of (the company of) those nearest to Allah...She said: "O my Lord! How shall I have a son when no man hath touched me?" He said: "Even so: Allah createth what He willeth: when He hath decreed a plan, He but saith to it 'Be', and it is!"...The similitude of Jesus before Allah is as that of Adam; He created him from dust, then said to him: "Be": and he was. (*Qur'an* 3:42, 45, 47, 59)

As to Jesus being the son of God in any literal sense, the *Qur'an* adamantly rejects such a possibility, just as did the aforementioned Christian saints, theologians, and bishops.

> It is not befitting to (the majesty of) Allah that He should beget a son. Glory be to Him! When He determines

a matter, He only says to it, "Be," and it is. (*Qur'an* 19:35)

16

Trinity

By Jerald F. Dirks, M.Div., Psy.D

INTRODUCTION

"You just have to take it on faith. It's a divine mystery, and human reason and logic cannot comprehend it." Those are never very satisfactory answers to the devout seeker of religious truth. Yet, almost any discussion of the trinity inevitably boils down to the proponent of this doctrine having to resort to the above statements.

In all fairness, there is probably no doctrine in all of Christianity as difficult to fathom in any meaningful way as that of the trinity. Attempts to discuss the trinity in any depth inevitably become bogged down in fruitless efforts to specify the interrelationships of the "three in one." How does the Father relate to the Son and the Holy Spirit? Which parts of the trinity proceeded from what other parts? Which parts of the trinity, if any, are subservient to the other parts? Which parts of the trinity did what in divine history, e.g., which part created the universe? The more one delves into such questions, the more one has to fall back on escape from reason by claiming that the doctrine is a "divine and ineffable mystery." Needless to say, this state of confusion is hardly a satisfactory conclusion, and appears to contradict the following Biblical verse.

For God is not the author of confusion...
(*I Corinthians* 14:33)

A PROBLEM WITH THE TRINITY

Traditional Christianity portrays the virgin birth of Jesus in terms of Jesus being the "begotten" son of God. For example, *Matthew* 1:18 states that Mary was "with child of the Holy Ghost", and *Luke* 1:35 has an angel telling Mary that the "Holy Ghost shall come upon thee". While these Biblical verses may be seen as rather ambiguous by some, the Nicene Creed of Christianity allows for no such ambiguity when it states: "We believe in one Lord, Jesus Christ, the only Son of God, eternally begotten of the Father, God from God, Light from Light, true God from true God, begotten, not made, one in Being with the Father." Further, the so-called Apostles' Creed holds that: "I believe in God the Father Almighty; maker of heaven and earth; and in Jesus Christ his only Son, our Lord; who was conceived by the Holy Ghost..."

As can be seen from the above listing of *New Testament* verses and creedal formulations, one of the fundamental problems confronting the Christian concept of the trinity is trying to decide whether the alleged father of Jesus Christ is the Father or the Holy Spirit. *Matthew* 1:18 says that Mary was "with child of the Holy Ghost," not the Father. *Luke* 1:35 says that Mary was told that the "Holy Ghost shall come upon thee," not the Father. The Apostles' Creed says that Jesus Christ was the Father's "only Son," but "was conceived by the Holy Ghost." Even the Nicene Creed, which says that Jesus was "begotten of the Father," goes on to say that Jesus "was incarnate from the Holy Spirit." So who was the father of Jesus Christ? Was it the Father or the Holy Spirit?

NO BIBLICAL BASIS FOR TRINITY

Given the confusion regarding the trinity, one does well to ask where and how the doctrine of the trinity ever originated. It certainly did not originate in the *Bible*, because the word "trinity" and its cognates and derivatives never appear in the text of the *Bible*—not even once! While there are a few scattered references in the *New Testament* to the Father, the Son, and the Holy Spirit, e.g., *Matthew* 28:19 and *1 John* 5:7, these passages can be shown to be later interpolations into the text of the *Bible*.

For example, the only part of *1 John* 5:7 that even exists in the oldest texts of the *Bible* is the phrase "(f)or there are three that bear record," which refers to the three witnesses described in the next verse. Analysis of Biblical texts indicates that the reference in *1 John* 5:7 to "the Father, the Word, and the Holy Ghost, and these three are one" first appeared in a *Bible* text in the fourth century, initially in Spain circa 380 and then later in the Latin Vulgate. As a few of the later Greek texts of the *Bible* have this fourth-century interpolation, it was picked up and included in the King James Version of the English *Bible*. In contrast, recent scholarly translations of the *Bible*, including the Revised Standard Version, the

New Revised Standard Version, and the Jerusalem Version, rightly omit this reference to "the Father, the Word, and the Holy Ghost" as being a late editorial insertion.

Furthermore, with regard to the "great commissioning" reported in *Matthew* 28:19, in which the "risen Jesus" reportedly told his disciples to baptize "in the name of the Father, and of the Son, and of the Holy Ghost," this can also be seen as a statement drawn from the early Christian church and not from the sayings of Jesus. As proof, one needs only note that *Acts* 2:38, 8:16, and 19:5 specifically state that the disciples of Jesus, the earliest Christians, and even Paul baptized in the name of Jesus, not in the name of the Father, Son, and Holy Ghost. Either all of them deliberately disobeyed Christ's order in the "great commissioning" or the order had never been given. Certainly, the latter appears to be the more realistic explanation. Furthermore, *Luke 24* claims that Jesus ascended into heaven on Easter Sunday and could thus not have been present to state what was recorded in *Matthew* 28:19.

THE BIBLICAL BASIS FOR UNITY

While there is no firm Biblical support for the doctrine of the trinity, the *Bible* is quite explicit in teaching the Unity and Oneness of God. For example, the *Shema* of the *Old Testament* is quite clear in rejecting any concept of the deity other than the Unity of God.

Hear, O Israel: The Lord our God is one... (*Deuteronomy* 6:4)

Further, the emphasis on the Unity of God is not limited to the *Old Testament* portion of the *Bible.* One also finds expression of the Unity and Oneness of God in the *New Testament.*

You believest that God is one; thou doest well: the devils also believe, and tremble. (*James* 2:19)

Furthermore, as reported by the *New Testament,* the Unity of God was also emphasized in the very words of Jesus Christ.

And one of the scribes came, and having heard them reasoning together, and perceiving that he had answered them well, asked him, Which is the first commandment of all? And Jesus answered him, The first of all the commandments is, Hear, O Israel; The Lord our God, the Lord is one... (*Mark* 12:28-29)

The above are only a few examples of the Unity of God recorded within the *Bible.* At the risk of belaboring the point, the following verses provide further Biblical support for the concept of the Unity of God.

Unto thee it was shewed, that thou mightest know that the Lord he is God; there is none else beside him. (*Deuteronomy* 4:35)

See now that I, even I, am he, and there is no god with me: I kill and I make alive; I wound, and I heal: neither is there any that can deliver out of my hand. (*Deuteronomy* 32:39)

That all the people of the earth may know that the Lord is God, and that there is none else. (*I Kings* 8:60)

Is there a God beside me? Yea, there is no God; I know not any...I am the Lord, and there is none else, there is no God beside me: I girded thee though thou hast not known me: That they may know from the rising of the sun, and from the west, that there is none beside me, I am the Lord, and there is none else...Tell ye, and bring them near; yea, let them take counsel together: who hath declared this from ancient time? Who hath told it from that time? Have not I the Lord? And there is no God else beside me; a just God and a Savior; there is none beside me. Look unto me, and be ye saved, all the ends of the earth: for I am God, and there is none else. (*Isaiah* 44:8b and 45:5-6, 21-22)

The reader is urged to note the constant and repetitious use of singular pronouns in referring to God in the above passages, not with the plural pronouns that would have been appropriate if there were "three in one."

THE DOCTRINE OF THE TRINITY

As should be clear by now, the doctrine of the trinity developed gradually over several centuries and not without substantial controversy and rejection.   Throughout its first several centuries, early Christianity struggled to maintain a strict monotheistic outlook, while still paying homage to God, Jesus Christ, and the Holy Spirit. One solution, represented primarily by the various Adoptionists (see the chapter entitled "Jesus: Man and God?") was to subordinate Jesus to God. A second solution, represented by modalism was to seek for some way of representing the Father, Jesus, and the Holy Spirit as simply three different functions or modes of self-disclosure of God, with there being no distinctive "persons" within the nature of God.

It was only with the Council of Nicaea in 325 that the doctrine that Jesus was of one substance with the Father began to be formulated in any real sense, although even at Nicaea, precious little was said about the Holy Spirit. Furthermore, there was little unity at Nicaea, and what there was occured only under the force of arms provided by Emperor Constantine. In reality, the Christian doctrine of the trinity was not really accepted until the Council of Constantinople in 381, at which time the Council concluded that the Holy Spirit was not subordinate to the Father and the Son, was a distinct "person" from the Father and the Son, but shared the same divine substance as the Father and the Son. As such, it was only towards the end of the fourth century that the traditional trinitarian concept of Christianity started to become "official" doctrine.

The Athanasian Creed of circa 500 states that God consists of *una substantia—tres personae* (one substance—three persons). But, the controversy was still far from over. As Augustine noted in *De Trinitate* (On the Trinity):

> ...our Greek friends have spoken of one essence (*ousia*) and three substances (*hypostases*), but the Latins of one essence or substance (*substantia*) and three persons (*personae*).

CONTINUING CONFLICT ABOUT THE TRINITY

The conflict regarding the trinity between Western or Latin Christianity and Eastern or Greek Christianity was not just confined to the issue of whether the trinity was three persons in one substance or three substances in one essence. Beginning in the sixth century, the Western Church gradually began to introduce the *Filioque* (and from the Son) clause into the Nicene Creed, directly following the words "the Holy Spirit...who proceedeth from the Father", thus rendering the Nicene Creed as "the Holy Spirit...who proceedeth from the Father and the Son". While the *Filioque* clause did not become official Roman Catholic doctrine until papal acceptance in the 11th century, the Eastern Church considered this insertion into the Nicene Creed to be a theological error. The Anglican Church and most Protestant churches have subsequently followed the lead of the Roman Catholic Church in accepting the *Filioque* clause.

This conflict over the insertion of the *Filioque* clause into Western Christianity's understanding of the trinity is not to be minimized. In at least partial response to this conflict, the Photian Schism of 867 divided Western and Eastern Christianity into two warring camps, with Pope Nicholas I refusing to acknowledge Photius as the bishop and patriarch of Constantinople and with Photius declaring Nicholas I deposed from the papacy. In 1054, the war between Western and Christianity reemerged. Once again, the *Filioque* clause was at least partially to blame. The end result was that Pope Leo IX excommunicated Michael Cerularius, the patriarch of Constantinople, on July 16, 1054. In quick response, Michael Cerularius excommunicated Pope Leo IX. Of note, these excommunications remained in place until lifted on December 7, 1965, by Pope Paul VI and Patriarch Athenagoras I.

How can a doctrine that results in the mutual excommunication of two of the highest leaders in Christianity be seen as anything other than mass confusion?

ISLAM AND THE NATURE OF GOD

One of the divides separating Islam from contemporary Christianity concerns the nature of God. Islam, like Judaism and several branches of early Christianity, teaches a strict and uncompromising monotheism, with God being seen as One and Indivisible. The *Qur'an* is most adamant in insisting on *Tawheed* (Oneness of God).

> O People of the Book! Commit no excesses in your religion; nor say of God anything but the truth. Christ Jesus ,the son of Mary, was (no more than) a messenger of God, and His word, which He bestowed on Mary, and a spirit proceeding from Him so believe in God and His messengers, do not say "Trinity," desist. It will be better for you, for God is One God. Glory be to Him:, (far exalted is He) above having a son. To Him belong all things in the heavens and on earth. And enough is God as a disposer of affairs. (*Qur'an* 4:171)

In blasphemy indeed are those who say that God is Christ, the son of Mary. ... They do blaspheme who say, "God is Christ, the son of Mary." But, said Christ:

"O children of Israel! Worship God, my Lord and your Lord." If anyone joins other gods with God, God will forbid him the garden, and the fire will be his abode. There will for the wrongdoers be no one to help. They do blaspheme who say, "God is one of three in a trinity" for there is no god except One God. (*Qur'an* 5:17a, 72-73a)

Say: He is God, the One and Only; God, the Eternal, Absolute; He does not beget, nor is He begotten; and there is none like Him. (*Qur'an* 112:1-4)

17

Vicarious Atonement in the "Blood of the Lamb"

By Jerald F. Dirks, M.Div., Psy.D.

INTRODUCTION

The doctrine of vicarious atonement has taken different forms in Western (Roman Catholic and Protestant) and Eastern (Orthodox) Christianity. In Eastern Christianity, salvation is usually seen as being the gift of immortality and holiness granted to man by God as a consequence of Christ's victory over death in his Easter resurrection. In contrast, Western Christianity has typically emphasized Christ's death on the cross as being expiation for the sins of mankind and as reconciling God and man following an estrangement that had existed ever since "Adam's initial fall from grace" by eating the forbidden fruit. Given this distinction, the concept of vicarious atonement in the "blood of the lamb" finds its fullest expression in Western Christianity.

WESTERN CHRISTIANITY AND VICARIOUS ATONEMENT

Little Biblical support for the doctrine of vicarious atonement can be found in the *New Testament* gospels, and what exists is quite ambiguous in content and meaning (e.g., *Mark* 10:45 & 14:22-24; and *John* 1:29). Thus, it is primarily in the *New Testament* epistles that one finds the Biblical basis for vicarious atonement, the basic points of which are as follows.

1) All mankind are sinners who have fallen short of salvation and the mercy and grace of God (*Romans* 3:23). 2) In part, we are all hopeless sinners and must die and be punished, because we have "inherited" the Original Sin of Adam (*Genesis* 3:1-19; *Romans* 5:12). 3) Believing in God and following His laws and commandments is insufficient for salvation (*Galatians* 2:15-21 & 3:10a). 4) Christ died upon the cross as a blood sacrifice for our sins and to relieve us of the burden of Original Sin (*Romans* 3:23-25 & 5:8; *Hebrews* 10:10; *I Corinthians* 15:3 & 11:24-25; *I Thessalonians* 5:9-10; *I Peter* 2:24 & 3:18; and *I John* 1:7). 5) Through the blood sacrifice of Christ Jesus, we are reconciled to God (*Romans* 5:12-14; *I Peter* 3:18) and relieved from the duty to follow the Mosaic Law (*Galatians* 3:10-13; *Romans* 3:28 & 7:6), so long as we believe in the alleged sacrifice on the cross of Jesus.

As can be seen from the above, the doctrine of vicarious atonement is based upon a series of assumptions, including: 1) that Jesus Christ was actually crucified, 2) that the crucifixion was part of the divine mission of Jesus, 3) that man was hopelessly estranged from God due to Adam's Original Sin, 4) that following the divine law was insufficient, and 5) that only a vicarious and intercessory sacrifice could reconcile God back to man. Each of these assumptions is examined in turn.

THE CRUCIFIXION EVENT

Outside of the *New Testament*, there appear to be only two references to Jesus being crucified in the entire historical record of the first century. The first was made by Josephus bin Matthias, a first century Jewish historian, and the second by Tacitus, a first and second century Roman. Neither writer was a witness to the crucifixion event. For that matter, most Biblical scholars maintain that none of the *New Testament* authors who wrote about the crucifixion event were witnesses to the crucifixion. Nonetheless, the typical Christian will rightly insist that any attempt to question the crucifixion of Jesus must marshal an impressive array of documentation that there was serious controversy about whether or not Jesus was actually crucified. "Where is that documentation?" they may well ask. Although it may come as a shock to most Christians, the answer is that it is to be found within the writings of early Christianity itself.

The writings of the Apostolic Fathers frequently noted that there were Christian sects that rejected the proposition that Jesus had been crucified. Such references can be found in the writings of Ignatius, Polycarp, Justin, Irenaeus, Tertullian, and Hippolytus. As a specific example, we can turn to

Trallians, a book authored by Ignatius, the bishop of Antioch, who died circa 110.

Ignatius wrote that there were Christians of his day who denied that Jesus was crucified in reality and maintained that he was crucified only in appearance or in illusion. Ignatius could not have been attacking a belief among early Christians that did not in fact already exist. His attack against those early Christians who believed that Jesus's crucifixion was only illusory demonstrates the existence of that belief among early Christians as early as 110, i.e., by the time of Ignatius's death. Further, the fact that Ignatius even bothered to attack this doctrine suggests that the belief in the illusory nature of the crucifixion was quite widespread by 110.

In addition, careful research uncovers several apocryphal books once accepted by early Christianity stating that it was not Jesus Christ who was crucified. For example, the *Apocalypse of Peter* 81:4-82:33 maintained that Jesus was crucified only in appearance, not in reality, with the one who was crucified being a substitute or simulacrum of Jesus. Likewise, the *Second Treatise of the Great Seth* 55:10-56:25 stated that it was not Jesus who was crucified, but Simon (presumably Simon of Cyrene, who is identified in *Matthew* 27:32, *Mark* 15:21, and *Luke* 23:26 as being the person who carried Christ's cross for him) and that Simon appeared as though he were Jesus. This position, i.e., that it was Simon of Cyrene who was crucified in place of Jesus, was a cardinal tenet of the early Christian group known as Basilideans, which flourished in Egypt during the second century and which claimed to be based directly on the teachings of Glaucias, the alleged interpreter of Peter, the disciple of Jesus Christ. Additionally, the *Acts of John* 97-101 reported that the crucifixion of Jesus was an illusion.[1]

It is not just within the so-called apocryphal writings that one finds evidence that it was not Jesus who was crucified. *Matthew* 27:11-26 states that Pontius Pilate, the Roman governor of Judea, gave the crowd a choice between releasing "Jesus who is called the Messiah" or "Jesus Barabbas." (Any Christians who might wonder about the name "Jesus Barabbas" are urged to consult the New Revised Standard Version of *Matthew* 27:17 for this identification, which is based on some of the oldest surviving texts of this verse.) *Matthew* then goes on to state that the crowd chose Jesus Barabbas and that Pilate released Jesus Barabbas. Of note, Barabbas, i.e., "*bar Abbas*," is not a given name, but is a patronymic, that is, a statement that one is the son of so-and-so. Translating from the Aramaic language, the language spoken by Jesus, "*bar Abbas*" may be translated as "son of the father." In short, *Matthew* tells the discerning reader that Pilate released "Jesus, the son of the Father" and condemned a different Jesus who was claiming to be the Messiah, i.e., the anointed one. The Hebrew word from which the Anglicized "Messiah" is derived means "anointed one." The anointed ones of Israel were the kings of Israel, the high priests of Israel, and some of the prophets of Israel. It can thus be cogently argued that the condemned prisoner was a Jesus who was a revolutionary and who was claiming to be the king of Israel, while the Jesus who was released was the "son of the Father." The name Jesus is the Greek rendition of Joshua, which was a fairly common name at that time.

So, who was who? Does this help explain why Pontius Pilate was canonized as a saint by the Coptic Christian Church? Does one justify sainthood for the man who condemned Jesus or for the man who released him? Certainly, *Matthew* raises the very real question of who was actually released and who was actually crucified.

THE MISSION OF JESUS

If Jesus was not crucified, what does this say about the Christian doctrine of the atonement in the blood? After all, was not the crucifixion of Jesus the crowning pinnacle of his divine mission? Was it not an absolutely indispensable part of his divine work? In addressing these questions, one has only to turn to the *New Testament* to discover what Jesus reportedly had to say about these very questions. His answer appears to be reported in a prayer attributed to Jesus in the gospel of *John*. Of decided importance, *John* places this prayer prior to the crucifixion event.

> And this is life eternal, that they might know thee the only God, and Jesus Christ, whom thou hast sent. I have glorified thee on the earth: I have finished the work which thou gavest me to do. (*John* 17:3-4)

"I ... finished the work that You gave me to do" and did so prior to the crucifixion event. As reported by *John*, Jesus specifically excluded the later crucifixion event and alleged resurrection as being part of his "work which thou gavest me to do." This would also negate any possibility that the "atonement in the blood" was in any manner part of the mission or work of Jesus Christ.

Of some interest with regard to this last point, Origen, perhaps the greatest Christian theologian of the third century, specifically rejected the concept that salvation came through the alleged crucifixion of Jesus and stressed that salvation was solely contingent upon man's proper exercise of his own free will, i.e., by proper belief and action.

ORIGINAL SIN

The doctrine of Original Sin is a completely Western Christian concept, which is primarily drawn from a rather idiosyncratic interpretation of *Romans* 5:12-19 and is based on the assumption that every human inherits the sin of "Adam's initial fall from grace" through conception via the act of sexual intercourse, an act that according to St. Augustine was contaminated by "concupiscence." Thus, according to traditional Western Christianity, the whole of mankind inherits Adam's Original Sin in eating of the forbidden fruit through being conceived through the sexual act. It should be emphasized at this point that the inheritance and concept of Original Sin are completely contrary to the religious teachings of Eastern Christianity, Judaism, and Islam, but are indigenous to Western Christianity.

As typically portrayed in Western Christian literature, "Adam's initial fall from grace" was a cataclysmic event, resulting in the following severe punishments that have accrued upon all humans ever since: 1) Adam and Eve were thrown out of the Garden of Eden and were forever barred from returning to it (*Genesis* 3:22-24); 2) Adam and his male descendants were specifically punished by being forced to till the "cursed" ground in order to find sustenance through "toil" and "the sweat of your face" (*Genesis* 3:17-19); 3) Eve and her female descendants were punished by the physical pain of childbirth and by having their husbands forever rule over them (*Genesis* 3:16); 4) All of humanity is punished by having to undergo death at the end of their lives in the earthly world (*Genesis* 3:22-24).

According to traditional Christian doctrine, "Adam's initial fall from grace" was not directly attributable to any moral or spiritual failing in Adam but was specifically secondary to the ethical and religious turpitude of Eve, who having been deceived by Satan, then deceived her husband. Had it not been for Eve, Adam would never have fallen from grace. Thus, all the toil and suffering of humanity ever since that first fateful bite of the forbidden fruit can be laid directly at the doorstep of Eve and through her to all women.

> For Adam was first formed, then Eve. And Adam was not deceived, but the woman being deceived was in the transgression. Notwithstanding she shall be saved in childbearing, if they continue in faith and charity and holiness with sobriety. (*I Timothy* 2:13-15)

Eve deceived Adam, who was her moral and spiritual superior. It was Eve who succumbed to the temptations of Satan, not Adam. As such, Eve's only hope for salvation, and after Eve for all women, was through undergoing the penance of the aforementioned physical pain of childbirth. But, the above verses from *I Timothy* are only the start of the process by which Western Christianity has traditionally attempted to lay the blame for all of the sins of humanity upon women. The Western Christian concept of women being to blame for Original Sin was further elaborated by the saints and theologians of early Western Christianity, such as Tertullian (*De Cultu Feminarum*) and St. Augustine (*Enchyridion*, chapter 26; letter #243; and *The Literal Meaning of Genesis*.)

Despite *Romans* 5:12-19 and the thinking of early theologians in Western Christianity, there are a number of Biblical references that cast severe doubt on there being any basis for a doctrine of Original Sin.

> The fathers shall not be put to death for the children, neither shall the children be put to death for the fathers: every man shall be put to death for his own sin. (*Deuteronomy* 24:16)

> The soul that sinneth, it shall die. The son shall not bear the iniquity of the father, neither shall the father bear the iniquity of the son: the righteousness of the righteous shall be upon him, and the wickedness of the wicked shall be upon him. But if the wicked will turn from all his sins that he hath committed, and keep all my statutes, and do that which is lawful and right, he shall surely live, he shall not die. (*Ezekiel* 18:20-21)

Furthermore, reason dictates that we will not be held accountable and judged on the basis of what our original progenitor did. Basic fairness allows no other conclusion.

FREED FROM THE LAW

As seen previously, Paul was at great pains to stress that the crucifixion event freed mankind from following the dictates of the divine law. But Paul's position stands in sharp contrast to the reported words of Jesus Christ.

Think not that I am come to destroy the law, or the prophets: I am not come to destroy, but to fulfill. For verily I say unto you, Till heaven and earth pass, one jot or one tittle shall in no wise pass from the law, till all be fulfilled. Whosoever therefore shall break one of these least commandments, and shall teach men so, he shall be called the least in the kingdom of heaven... (*Matthew* 5:17-19a)

...keep the commandments. (*Matthew* 19:17)

And it is easier for heaven and earth to pass, than one tittle of the law to fail. (*Luke* 16:17)

INTERCESSORY SACRIFICE

Can one actually be sacrificed for the sins of another? The following Biblical verses would appear to answer negatively and stress that each person must pay the price for his own sins.

The fathers shall not be put to death for the children, neither shall the children be put to death for the fathers: every man shall be put to death for his own sin. (*Deuteronomy* 24:16)

...it is only the person who sins that shall die. (*Ezekiel* 18:4b)

The soul that sinneth, it shall die. The son shall not bear the iniquity of the father, neither shall the father bear the iniquity of the son: the righteousness of the righteous shall be upon him, and the wickedness of the wicked shall be upon him. But if the wicked will turn from all his sins that he hath committed, and keep all my statutes, and do that which is lawful and right, he shall surely live, he shall not die. All his transgressions that he hath committed, they shall not be mentioned unto him: in his righteousness that he hath done he shall live. (*Ezekiel* 18:20-22)

Moreover, Jesus appeared to be rejecting intercessory sacrifice for sins when he reportedly taught that the path to salvation was by keeping the commandments.

...but whosoever shall do and teach them, the same shall be called great in the kingdom of heaven. (*Matthew* 5:19b)

And, behold, one came and said unto him, Good Master, what good thing shall I do, that I may have eternal life? And he said unto him, Why callest thou me good? There is none good but one, that is, God: but if thou wilt enter into life, keep the commandments. (*Matthew* 19:16-17)

A HYPOTHETICAL EXAMPLE

Consider the following hypothetical example. Some

people have done you a wrong. That wrong is so grievously distressing to you that you cannot find it in your heart ever to forgive them. You simply have no mercy left for those who have wronged you. But you do send your son to them to admonish them. In response, these same people kill your son in the most gruesome of ways. As a result of your son's suffering and death at the hands of these people, you are now overcome with love and mercy for them, so you are finally able to forgive them. You are now able to forgive them, because they have killed your son. Does such a scenario really make any sense whatsoever? Yet, that is exactly what the doctrine of vicarious atonement in the "blood of the lamb" is all about.

THE ISLAMIC PERSPECTIVE

As can be seen from the above review, each and every one of the assumptions underlying the doctrine of vicarious atonement is a shaky foundation at best. As such, it is perhaps time to present what Islam has to say about these issues.

Like many early Christians, Islam rejects the idea that Jesus Christ was crucified. The basis of this rejection is found in the *Qur'an.*

> That they said (in boast), "We killed Christ Jesus the son of Mary, the messenger of Allah"— but they did not kill him, nor crucified him, but so it was made to appear to them, and those who differ therein are full of doubts, with no (certain) knowledge, but only conjecture to follow, for of a surety they did not kill him —nay, Allah raised him up unto Himself; and Allah is exalted in

power, wise (*Qur'an* 4:157-158)

Like Judaism and Eastern Christianity, Islam rejects the concept of Original Sin. But, Islam goes even further and teaches that Adam and Eve were equally culpable when it came to eating of the forbidden fruit, thus totally negating the basis for the degradation of women found in Western Christianity. This can be seen by noting the plural pronouns in the following verse.

Then did Satan make them slip from the (garden), and get them out of the state (of felicity) in which they had been. (*Qur'an* 2:36a)

Moreover, the *Qur'an* specifically states that God forgave Adam for his initial transgression, thus removing any sin that could possibly be inherited — as though such an inheritance were possible.

Then learned Adam from his Lord words of inspiration, and his Lord turned towards him; for He is oft-returning, most merciful. (*Qur'an* 2:37)

Finally with regard to Original Sin, both the *Qur'an* and the sayings of Prophet Muhammad reject the concept that babies are born into sin.

We have indeed created man in the best of moulds. (*Qur'an* 95:4)

It is reported on the authority of Abu Mu'awiya that (the Holy Prophet) said: "Every new-born babe is born on the millat (of Islam and he) remains on this until his tongue is enabled to express himself." (*Muslim, Hadith*

#6427)

The *Qur'an* also stresses that each person will be held accountable for his own behavior, that no other can bear the burden of sinful behavior that one has accumulated, and that intercessory salvation is a forlorn hope.

Namely, that no bearer of burdens can bear the burden of another; that man can have nothing but what he strives for; that (the fruit of) his striving will soon come in sight; then will he be rewarded with a reward complete... (*Qur'an* 53:38-41)

On that Day shall no intercession avail except for those for whom permission has been granted by (Allah) most gracious and whose word is acceptable to Him. (*Qur'an* 20:109)

Again, what will explain to you what the Day of Judgment is? (It will be) the Day when no soul shall have power (to do) anything for another, for the command, that Day, will be (wholly) with Allah. (*Qur'an* 82:18-19)

Within Islam, salvation is seen as being contingent upon a person's belief in the absolute Oneness and Unity of God. But, faith without works is insufficient. Given that a correct monotheistic belief is present, final judgment is based upon a weighing of each person's behavior and intentions throughout life. Fortunately for all concerned, this weighing is heavily tempered by the abundant mercy of God.

He that does good shall have ten times as much to his

credit: he that does evil shall only be recompensed according to his evil. No wrong shall be done unto (any of) them. (*Qur'an* 6:160)

Notes:

[1] For a fuller discussion of these issues, as well as for the text of the cited passages from the various books of the *New Testament* apocrypha, see Dirks JF: *The Cross and the Crescent*. Beltsville, Amana Publications, 2001. Chapter 5.

Muhammad in the Bible

By Dr. Jamal Badawi

"Those who follow the Apostle, the unlettered Prophet, Whom they find mentioned in their own Scriptures, in the Torah, and the Gospel... " (Qur'an 7:157 trans: Yusif Ali]

BIBLE PROPHECIES ABOUT THE ADVENT OF MUHAMMAD

Abraham is widely regarded as the common father of the Jews, Christians, and Muslims. Through his second son, Isaac, came all Israelite prophets including such towering figures as Jacob, Joseph, Moses, David, Solomon and Jesus. May peace and blessings be upon them all. The advent of these great prophets was in partial fulfillment of God's promises to bless the nations of the earth through the descendants of Abraham (Genesis 12:2-3). Such fulfillment is wholeheartedly accepted by Muslims whose faith considers the belief in and respect for all prophets an article of faith.

BLESSINGS OF ISHMAEL AND ISAAC

Were the first-born son of Abraham (Ishmael) and his descendants included in God's covenant and promise? A few verses from the Bible may help shed some light on this question;

1) Genesis 12:2-3 speaks of God's promise to Abraham and his descendants before any child was born to him.

2) Genesis 17:4 reiterates God's promise after the birth of Ishmael and before the birth of Isaac.

3) In Genesis, ch. 21, Isaac is specifically blessed but Ishmael was also specifically blessed and promised by God to become "a great nation," especially in Genesis 21:13, 18.

4) According to Deuteronomy 21:15-17, the traditional rights and privileges of the first-born son are not to be affected by the social status of his mother (being a "free" women such as Sarah, Isaac's mother, or a "bondwoman" such as Hagar, Ishmael's mother). This is only consistent with the moral humanitarian principles of all revealed faiths.

5) The full legitimacy of Ishmael as Abraham's son and "seed" and the full legitimacy of his mother, Hagar, as Abraham's wife are clearly stated in Genesis 21:13 and 16:3.

After Jesus, the last Israelite messenger and prophet, it was time that God's promise to bless Ishmael and his descendants be fulfilled. Less than 600 years after

Jesus, came the last messenger of God, Muhammad, from the progeny of Abraham through Ishmael. God's blessing of both of the main branches of Abraham's family tree was now fulfilled. But, is there additional corroborating evidence that the Bible did in fact foretell the advent of prophet Muhammad?

MUHAMMAD: THE PROPHET LIKE UNTO MOSES

A long time after Abraham, God's promise to send the long-awaited messenger was repeated this time in Moses's words.

In Deuteronomy 18:18, Moses spoke of the prophet to be sent by God who is:

1) From among the Israelite's "brethren," a reference to their Ishmaelite cousins as Ishmael was the other son of Abraham who was explicitly promised to become a "great nation."

2) A prophet like unto Moses. There were hardly any two prophets who were so much alike as Moses and Muhammad. Both were given a comprehensive law and code of life, both encountered their enemies and were victors in miraculous ways, both were accepted as prophets/statesmen and both migrated following conspiracies to assassinate them. Analogies between Moses and Jesus overlook not only the above similarities but other crucial ones as well (e.g. the natural birth, family life, and death of Moses and Muhammad but not Jesus, who was regarded by His followers as the Son of God and not exclusively a messenger of God, as Moses and Muhammad were

and as Muslims believe Jesus was).

Deuteronomy 33:1-2 combines references to Moses, Jesus, and Muhammad. It speaks of God (i.e., God's revelation) coming from Sinai, rising from Seir (probably the village of Sa'ir near Jerusalem) [1] and shining forth from Paran. According to Genesis 21:21, the wilderness of Paran was the place where Ishmael settled (i.e. Arabia, specifically Mecca). Indeed the King James version of the Bible mentions the pilgrims passing through the valley of Ba'ca (another name of Mecca) in Psalms 84:4-6.

Isaiah 42:1-13 speaks of the beloved of God. His elect and messenger who will bring down a law to be awaited in the isles and who "shall not fail nor be discouraged till he have set judgment on earth." Verse 11, connects that awaited one with the descendants of Ke'dar. Who is Ke'dar? According to Genesis 25:13, Ke'dar was the second son of Ishmael, the ancestor of prophet Muhammad.

MUHAMMAD'S MIGRATION FROM MECCA TO MEDINA: PROPHESIED IN THE BIBLE?

Habakkuk 3:3 speaks of God (God's help) coming from Te'man (an oasis north of Medina according to J. Hasting's Dictionary of the Bible) and the holy one (coming) from Paran. That holy one who under persecution migrated from Paran (Mecca) to be received enthusiastically in Medina was none but

Prophet Muhammad.

Indeed the incident of the migration of the Prophet and his persecuted followers is vividly described in Isaiah 21:13-17. That section foretold as well about the battle of Badr in which the few ill-armed faithful miraculously defeated the "mighty" men of Ke'dar, who sought to destroy Islam and intimidate their own folks who turned to Islam.

THE QURAN (KORAN) FORETOLD IN THE BIBLE?

Muslims believe that God's words (the Qur'an) were truly put into Muhammad's mouth for twenty-three years. He was not the "author" of the Qur'an. The Qur'an was dictated to him by Angel Gabriel who asked Muhammad to simply repeat the words of the Qur'an as he heard them. These words were then committed to memory and to writing by those who heard them during Muhammad's life time and under his supervision.

Was it a coincidence that the prophet "like unto Moses" from the "brethren" of the Israelites (i.e. from the Ishmaelites) was also described as one in whose mouth God will put his words and that he will speak in the name of God., (Deuteronomy 18:18-20)? Was it also a coincidence the "Paraclete" that Jesus foretold to come after him was described as one who "shall not speak of himself, but whatsoever he shall hear, that shall he speak"? (John 16:13).

Was it another coincidence that Isaiah connects the messenger associated with Ke'dar with a new song (a scripture in a new language) to be sung unto the lord (Isaiah 42:10-11). More explicitly, Isaiah prophesies that this coming prophet "with stammering lips, and another tongue, will he speak to this people" (Isaiah 28:11). This latter verse correctly describes the "stammering lips" of Prophet Muhammad reflecting the state of tension and concentration he went through at the time of revelation. Another related point is that the Qur'an was revealed in piece-meal over a span of twenty three years. It is interesting to compare this with Isaiah 28:10 which speaks of the same thing.

THAT PROPHET-PARACLETE-MUHAMMAD

Up to the time of Jesus, the Israelites were still waiting for that prophet like unto Moses prophesied in Deuteronomy 18:18. When John the Baptist came, they asked him if he was Christ, and he said, "No." They asked him if he was Elias, and he said, "No." Then, in apparent reference to Deuteronomy 18:18, they asked him "art thou that Prophet" and he answered, "no" (John 1:19-21).

In the gospel according to John (Chapters 14, 15, 16) Jesus spoke of the "Paraclete" or comforter who will come after him, who will be sent by the Father as another Paraclete, who will teach new things which the contemporaries of Jesus could not bear. While the Paraclete is described as the spirit of truth, (whose meaning resembles Muhammad's famous title Al-Amin, the trustworthy), he is identified in one verse as the Holy Ghost (John 14:26). Such a designation, however, is inconsistent with the profile of that Paraclete. In the words of the Dictionary of the Bible (Ed. J. Mackenzie), "These items, it must be admitted do not give an entirely coherent picture." Indeed, history tells us that many early Christians understood the Paraclete to be a man and not a spirit. This might explain the followers who responded to some who claimed, without meeting the criteria stipulated by Jesus, to be the awaited "Paraclete."

It was Prophet Mohammed who was the Paraclete, comforter, helper, admonisher sent by God after Jesus. He testified about Jesus and taught new things that could not be borne at Jesus's time, he spoke what he heard (revelation), and he dwells with the believers (through his well-preserved teachings). Such teachings will remain forever because he was the last messenger of God, the only Universal Messenger to unite the whole of humanity under God and on the path of PRESERVED truth. He told of many things to come, which "came to pass," in the minutest detail, meeting the criterion given by Moses to distinguish between the true prophet and the false prophets (Deuteronomy 18:22). He did reprove the world of sin, of righteousness and of judgment (John 16:8-11).

WAS THE SHIFT OF RELIGIOUS LEADERSHIP PROPHESIED?

Following the rejection of the last Israelite prophet, Jesus, it was about time for God's promise to make Ishmael a great nation to be fulfilled (Genesis 21:13, 18). In Matthew 21:19-21, Jesus spoke of the fruitless fig tree (a Biblical symbol of prophetic heritage) to be cleared after being given a last chance of three years (the duration of Jesus's ministry) to give fruit. In a later verse in the same chapter, Jesus said: "Therefore, say I unto you, The Kingdom of God shall be taken from you, and given to a nation bringing forth the fruits thereof" (Matthew 21:43). That nation was Ishmael's descendants (the rejected stone in Matthew 21:42) who were victorious against all super-powers of their time as prophesied by Jesus: "And whosoever shall fall on this stone shall be broken, but on whomsoever it shall fall, it will grind him to powder" (Matthew 21:44).

OUT OF CONTEXT COINCIDENCE?

Is it possible that the numerous prophecies cited here are all individually and combined out of context misinterpretations? Is the opposite true, that such infrequently studied verses fit together consistently and clearly point to the advent of the man who changed the course of human history, Prophet Muhammad? Is it reasonable to conclude that all these prophecies, appearing in different books of the Bible and spoken by various prophets at different times, were all coincidental? If this is so, here is another strange "coincidence"!

One of the signs of the prophet to come from Paran (Mecca) is that he will come with "ten thousands of saints" (Deuteronomy 33:2 KJV). That was the number of faithful who accompanied Prophet Muhammad to Paran (Mecca) in his victorious, bloodless return to his birthplace to destroy the remaining symbols of idolatry in the Ka'bah.

Says God as quoted by Moses:

And it shall come to pass, that whosoever will not hearken unto my words which he shall speak in my name, I will require it of him (Deuteronomy 18:19).

Endnotes:

[1] Compiler's note: Other commentary suggests Seir (Mt. Seir) to be in the vicinity of what is today Petra, Jordan.

Section IV: Other Topics

In the Name of God, Most Gracious, Most Merciful
Say: He is God the One and Only;
God the Eternal Absolute;
He does not beget, nor is He begotten;
And there is none like Him.

Quran Surah Al-Ikhlass

Islam & the Environment

By F. Kamal

What is expected of a viceroy, a trustee or ruler? If those over whom one commands power are killed without cause, have their homes polluted heedlessly with toxic wastes, and have deformities and diseases resulting from the careless and wasteful disposal of carcinogens, should not the ruler be asked if he is discharging his responsibilities and trust faithfully? Unfortunately, there have been altogether too many shameful, unnecessary cases of pollution that have taken their toll on the planet, the animals, and the plants that inhabit it. One wonders if man is taking his responsibilities seriously.

> Quran 2:30 "...Your Lord said unto the angels: "Lo! I am about to place a viceroy on the earth...," and Quran 22:65 "Do you not see that God has made subject to you (humans) all that is on the earth"

In Islam, Muslims believe that man has been given a responsibility by Allah (i.e., Arabic for God) on this earth and that man will be accountable to God for his actions and the trust placed in him. Prophet Muhammad said, "Everyone of you is a guardian and is responsible for his charges. The ruler who has authority over people is a guardian and is responsible for them" (*Sahih Bukhari 3.46.730*). Islam has urged humanity to be kind to nature and not to abuse the trust that has been placed on the shoulders of man. In fact, to be kind to animals is an integral part of Islam for Muslims. There are two primary sources defining Islam: The Quran (Muslim Holy Book) and the Hadith (the example, sayings, and actions of Prophet Muhammad). Both emphasize the accountability and responsibility of man toward the rest of creation.

Prophet Muhammad announced the rewards of caring for animals and the importance of avoiding cruelty to animals. He urged kindness toward all living things. He recounted a case of a women who was insensitive and cruel to her cat. She had kept locked up until it died of hunger. So God punished her for it on the Day of Judgement. "God said (to the woman), 'You neither fed it nor watered it when you locked it up, nor did you set it free to eat the insects of the earth." (Sahih Bukhari). This was 1400 years ago — long before it became fashionable or "politically correct" to care about "animal rights." Yet even in this barbaric time the Prophet had banned forcing animals to fight for human entertainment (*Sunan Abu Dawud #2556*).

In fact, there was no concept of "animal rights" or for that matter much civility by the strong toward the weak in the rough Arabian society that Prophet Muhammad had been born into more then 1400 years ago. He also talked of the great rewards of kindness to animals. He recounted, "While a man was walking he felt thirsty and went down a well and drank water from it. On coming out of it, he saw a dog panting and eating mud because of extreme thirst.

The man said, 'This (dog) is suffering from the same problem as I am.' So he (went down the well) filled his shoe with water, caught hold of it with his teeth, and climbed up and watered the dog. God thanked him for his (good) deed and forgave him." The people asked, "O God's Apostle! Is there a reward for us in serving (the) animals?" He replied, "Yes, there is a reward for serving any animate being." (*Sahih Bukhari 3.40.551*).   During the prophet's life, Muslims were instructed that one could not allow one's beasts of burden (camels) to become hungry (through neglect), or even to overburden them (by loading them too heavily). (Sunan Abu Dawud #2543).   These were radical ideas for that place and time.

Nature and environment have always played an important part in the lives of devout Muslims. Muslims understand that God has not created all this for nothing. In fact, Muslims have been commanded to find the wonderful signs of God around them so that they will only increase them in their awe of their Rabb (Cherisher and Sustainer).

Behold! in the creation of the heavens and the earth, and the alternation of night and day- there are indeed Signs for men of understanding men who celebrate the praises of God, standing, sitting, and lying down on their sides, and contemplate the (wonders of) creation in the heavens and the earth (with the thought): "Our Lord! not for nothing have You created (all) this! Glory to You! Give us salvation from the penalty of the Fire *Quran 3.190-1.*

Early Muslims intrinsically understood this and led the world in science. In fact. modern science owes much to Muslim scientists (see Islamic websites on this topic such as http://cyberistan.org/islamic/ for more details on this topic). But it was a science intertwined with seeking the Glory of God, not a cold pursuit devoid of any ethical considerations. It was not a confrontation with nature, but a search for God's signs, limitless bounty, and Mercy. It is in kindness that our Lord has reassured us through His prophet:

> The Prophet (peace be upon him) said: "God has sent down both the disease and the cure, and He has appointed a cure for every disease, so treat yourselves medically, but use nothing unlawful." (*Sunan Abu Dawud, book 28, number 3865*)

In fact, nature offers a rich bounty in the medicinal arena. Silver, for example, has potent germicidal properties (e.g., even capable of anti-microbial activities at which antibiotics fail) and has widely been used (e.g. silver sulphadiazine in burn centers in America), and iodine (e.g. tincture of iodine) is used as a disinfectant.

Medicine has also benefited greatly from the animal kingdom. Honey from bees has a number of medicinal uses. While maggots and leeches may conjure up discredited images of medieval medicine, one may be surprised to find that they have made a resurgence in modern medicine. Leeches have recently been used in microsurgery to control swelling in order to promote the healing necessary to reattach severed fingers, for example. Leeches conveniently provide an anticoagulant (e.g., hirudin or hementin—as in the Amazonian species), an anesthetic and some antibiotic properties through their saliva – all in one package. "Disinfected" maggots have been used in MDT (Maggot Debridement Therapy) to treat certain types of wound healing They release proteolytic enzymes to aid in debridement (removal of unwanted matter), enzymes with antimicrobial properties, and compounds like allantonin, urea, ammonium bicarbonate, and a calcium carbonate/picric acid mixture that seem to promote wound healing. Scientists have even managed to analyze snake venom. Pit viper and cobra venom can help make anticoagulant drugs. Work on the jararaca pit viper's venom has found use in hypertension drugs.

The plant kingdom too has paved the way for an extraordinary number of modern drugs. Aspirin, is probably one of our most famous modern drugs. Did you know it has its beginnings from the salicylic acid from the willow tree. How about quinine – from cinchona trees -- a treatment for malaria? It too has its origins in nature. Then there is the "miracle" antibiotic penicillin from the mold (fungus) penicillium, a medicine that has helped millions of people. How about digitalis from the foxglove plant, Ipecac (whooping cough), tuba/quassia (lice infestations), quabain (heart disease), curare (spastic ceberal palsy, tetanus convolutions, surgery aid), sangre de grado (stomach cancer/peptic ulcers), mangroves Curacin A (which may help combat breast and colon cancers) and epibatidine (painkiller) from the poison dart frog.

Today, important new fronts in medicine are being opened in molecular biology, biomedical engineering, human-machine interfaces, biochemistry, nanotechnology, ideas like rational drug design, advances in the genome project (and its successors), better understanding of things like RNAi, and emerging "biological hardware and software" possibilities.

Exponential increases in computing power are also allowing complex 3D calculations which model how molecules could fit together to identify possible candidates for medicines from a staggering field of combinational possibilities. Massive database coupled with processing power and emerging automated testing also allow for pattern matching disease/solution signatures.

But at the same time we are losing species to extinction, biodiversity is threatened, and human reservoirs of traditional medicinal knowledge are dwindling. Let us, for example, discuss biodiversity in conjunction with our stewardship of the land.

Many problems plague our stewardship of the land, but one bright spot is the "Svalbard Global Seed Vault." It is a giant vault meant to preserve earth's seed biodiversity.

Why does seed biodiversity matter? Human history has known terrible agricultural disasters in the past that resulted in massive famines. Our food harvests are vulnerable to drought, pests and plant disease. Consider the specter of a massive wheat harvest failure due to disease. Fortunately, we are not entirely helpless. Within the giant seed vault lies, for example, wheat seed variety PI178383. Once PI178383 was considered useless. Not a useable wheat seed for food.

But stored within its genes is a treasure trove of disease fighting tools. Such gene insights (e.g. bunt, stripe rust, and snow mold resistance genes) may be used to fortify food wheat crops against disease. Here is a important lesson, that something that appears useless today, may be incredibly valuable sometime in the future. We have unfortunately already lost a great deal of biodiversity, which may be lost for a long time, but in the "Svalbard Global Seed Vault" mankind is making a proud stand to halt the perilous loss of plant biodiversity. [1] This vault of seed biodiversity has locked in itself the secret shortcuts of tested, optimized solutions to all sorts of problems - some which we are undoubtedly not even aware of.

Perhaps as our past failure to manage biodivesity, handicap and delay our abilities to exploit and leverage fully our new technologies, we will begin to realize the true value of the enormous treasures we failed to appreciate and protect.

In addition to the domains of earth, plant and animal insights into engineering medical solutions, the environment can also help us handle human crime.

If one has an opportunity to watch videos of modern forensic entomology/biology (e.g. detective work using insect and plant evidence) Muslims marvel at how one can see evidence of the extraordinary Mercy of God — available for those who seek it. There have been cases of men being released from death penalty criminal prosecutions because simple insect evidence scientifically dated a crime to a time where it was impossible for the suspect to have committed the crime. Alternatively, vicious killers have been caught lying when their alibi statements clearly contradicted plant evidence.

Muslims note that God can be kind beyond words— if people exert their minds and hearts. ".... But if you count the favors of God, never will you be able to number them" Quran 14:34. His signs, Muslims feel, are everywhere.

Another important aspect to our stewardship of the land is managing pollution. One of the most destructive causes of pollution is consumer waste. Needless and wasteful consumer packaging, for example, unnecessarily fills up our landfills. Vast tracts of tropical rainforests – potentially the storehouse of numerous as-yet-undiscovered medicines – are heedlessly destroyed through neglect, mismanagement, laziness, greed and wasteful methodologies. When toxic chemicals are driven into our waters by greed, Muslims may reflect on what is written in Quran 30:41: "Corruption appears on land and sea because of (the evil) that men's hands have done, so that He may make them taste a part of what they have done, in order that they may return." Have our inner problems become our outer problems? Numerous animals and plants are thoughtlessly killed and harvested when people throw out tons of unused food. Yet some of these animals that end up in garbage cans may have had their numbers occasionally artificially inflated by production techniques that border on being inhumane or at least of questionable ethics in order to meet the huge consumer buying demands.

Lo! the squanderers were ever brothers of the devils, and the devil was ever an ingrate to his Lord. Quran 17.27.

Muslims have been enjoined to avoid waste and ingratitude to their Lord. Muslims strive to find the signs of God in nature to glorify their Lord, to thank Him, and to order their world in the manner in which their Rabb (Cherisher and Sustainer) wishes it to be ordered. They do not disorder their world in heedlessness of their Rabb in search of self-gratification, greed, and waste and with ingratitude to their Lord.

Yet even then within the plant world we find some possible solutions for the pollution we have created. For example, plants called hyperaccumulators can grow in polluted soil. A plant, Slender brake, pteris ensiformis, can "accumulate" heavy metals, such as zinc and cobalt from contaminated soils in a clean up process called "bio-remediation."

Plants may be used to clean the air. Lady palms may remove ammonia and formaldehyde from the air. Yellow poplar (e.g. tulip poplar) may reduce high soil levels of atrazine (a farm fertilizer). Hybrid poplar trees may pull up heavy metals and solvents in a process called phytoremediation. Phytoremediation offers the potential to restore soil health while cleansing it.

Finally, God reminds humanity about the beauty of his creatures for which He has entrusted the burden, responsibility, and accountability to man as His viceroy.

> Do they not look at the earth,-how many noble things of all kinds We have produced in it? Quran 26:7

Muslims seek God's help in discharging their responsibilities in a manner that pleases Him and to thank Him for the extraordinary bounties He has placed here.

The rewards of tending to the environment are great indeed.

> Anas reported God's Messenger as saying, "Whenever a Muslim plants trees or cultivates land and birds or a man or a beast eats out of them, it is a charity on his behalf." *Sahih Muslim book 010, number 3769*

Practicing Muslims see God's extraordinary beauty and bounties in such copious amounts around them that for the grateful heart God's Grace seems to know no limit. In fact, when faced with the seemingly infinite reservoir of Grace all Muslims can say is : "All praise is to God, Lord of the worlds."

Author's Note: When I have on occasion visited some

Muslim majority nations it has saddened me to see a sometimes cavalier (almost to a point of carelessness) attitude towards things like pollution. I really do understand that there is a lot of poverty and lack of education in these regions. But I know there are many good people there too, who if reminded of Islamic teachings, will strive for a more healthy relationship between man and his environment. Perhaps this article will help in that regard.

FURTHER READING

EXTERNALITIES

There is an interesting concept in modern economics called "externalities." It deals with certain market price imperfections arising due to poor information transmission. The transmission of information between individuals (who are immediate parties to a transaction) and others (who may not be immediate parties to a transaction) may be loosely coupled, leading to an inefficient allocation of costs and benefits between the parties.

A classic example of a negative externality is your neighbor deciding to sell his plot of land to be used as a "toxic dump" by a polluting company. While your neighbor has realized a handsome profit, the polluting company may not be paying the true cost of the transaction. The prices of homes in your neighborhood will plummet; increased cancer rates, medical costs, reduced longevity and productivity may also occur – and none of these costs will be assumed by the polluting company. Thus, the true cost to the nation is significantly higher than the actual cost paid by the polluting company.

Furthermore, if the national/state government pays medicare/medicaid or other federal/state medical payments that can be shown to be linked to the toxic dump, the government, in a sense, could be subsidizing the cost of the initial transaction for the polluting company. "Externalities" are an interesting area of modern economics with many important policy implications.

PUBLIC GOODS/GAME THEORY

In sociology there is a concept of "public goods." Examples of public goods could be oceans, public parks, or even portions of the electromagnetic spectrum. Research has delved into the conflict between self interest and the public interest. For example, oceans have a maximum clearing rate for their fishing stocks after which severe species depletion can occur. As long as fishers cooperate and do not over fish they can all prosper. This, however, is in perennial conflict with an individual's incentive to fish for maximum profit.

(Note: If you are interested in a closely related topic and are a teacher, you might want to check out the following teaching simulation called "Tragedy of the Commons Simulation" (Tori Haidinger. College board AP program). Search google.com or follow up with www.enviroliteracy.org/pdf/materials/1132.pdf)

Sociologists, such as Ostrom, have identified several factors that can cement cooperation among individuals. Factors include the importance of monitoring in order to assure that those subject to the rules play a role in developing them, that sanctions are graduated and that low cost methods exist to resolve conflicts. Game theory (the iterated prisoner's dilemma, tit for tat, reputation, and Fehr's and Gachter's public goods game) all attempt to tackle and illuminate the issues dealing with "public goods" and cooperation. [Note: Sometimes the words "the commons" is used with reference to this topic.]

JUSTICE

How can the study of nature help bring about justice? If you wish to encourage young people to consider careers in law enforcement and science check out PBS's video "Creatures in crime" and Vivien Bower's "Crime Science." For example, the last three chapters (each about 2-3 pages) in Ms. Bower's book deal with cases for a forensic botanist, a forensic geologist, and a forensic entomologist written for a young audience.

REAL LIFE CASE STUDIES

Real life environment cases are interesting studies since they illustrate societal dynamics, subtleties, pitfalls, and solutions. One intriguing case involves the disastrous cases of mercury poisoning in Minamata, Japan.

Other cases:

Elephants: Be realistic enough to identify and transform misdirected financial incentives with enough creativity and hard work to realign the financial incentives toward your goal. For example, elephants are killed in areas of abject poverty because of the realizable economic value of their tusks. Some individuals have sought to make elephants more valuable alive than dead by creating "photo safaris" where a portion of the proceeds benefit the local villagers. This paradigm shift has turned the profit motive on its head with promising results for both the elephants and local people.

Biodiversity: Another interesting case deals with the tension between the ranchers and biodiversity in the Amazon. Here too, attempts are being made to align tangible economic benefits with preserving biodiversity. For example, attempts are being made to link biodiversity goals with a realizable economic stake in pharmaceutical patents arising from research in Amazon plant species.

"Cap and trade": The history of acid rain and the climate control exchange both offer interesting reading. "Cap and trade" is an economic concept to transfer resources by penalizing less compliant solutions (that overshoot a "cap" threshold) and by rewarding and encouraging more promising environmental ones (e.g. those below the "cap" threshold). Climate control exchange may be interesting to follow (see also the rainforest coalition and carbon sequestration/emissions) to understand how economic techniques may be used impact perceived environmental issues.

Economic solutions should not be explored in a vacuum. In addition, to rigorous scientific research, science can often provide solutions to problems it "creates."

SCIENCE

Science can play an important, positive role in solving environmental puzzles. One such interesting case occurred in China, where individuals from a certain area were suffering serious heart problems. Scientists ultimately cracked this environmental conundrum with sampling and measuring techniques linking a deficit of selenium in the soil to the heart problems. Selenium supplements for those people solved their heart problems.

In almost the opposite scenario, in the early 1930s American dentist Charles MacKay from Colorado Springs, Colorado, who lived in an area with a statistically higher incidence of fluoride in the water, noticed the sharp decrease in cavities in the local population. Eventually, science was able to demonstrate a link between fluoride in the water and reduced cavities. Today, water municipalities regularly introduce minute quantities of fluoride to our drinking water in order to improve our dental health.

These days, scientists can use various scientific measuring techniques to monitor our environment. Titration techniques can check for water salinity, spectrophotometric absorbance can check for traces of mercury in solution, and emission spectroscopy can check for types and concentrations of elements and bonds that can be checked against known "fingerprints."

Endnotes:

[1]See http://www.cbsnews.com/stories/2008/
03/20/60minutes/main3954557.shtml and
http://www.ars-grin.gov/npgs/cgc_reports/1996_
wheatcgc_report.pdf

Disclaimer: Despite the best efforts of the author and publisher, this book may contain mistakes. As such the reader should not use this book as an ultimate reference, but rather cross check facts across several different works and with the appropriate professionals while independently engaging in their own due diligence. The reader is encouraged to explore and learn as much about the subject area as possible., Do not use this book as a source of, or substitute for, professional medical advice. Do not attempt to treat yourself medicinally. Seek qualified medical professionals to treat your medical problems. The author and publisher are not engaging in rendering medical services. Accordingly, the author and publisher expressly disclaim any liability, loss damage, or injury caused by the contents of this book..

Islam & Intoxicants

By F. Kamal

Intoxicants (Alcohol & Illegal Drugs) and Islam

Susan is victim of Fetal Alcohol Syndrome -- a birth defect she acquired because her mother drank while pregnant. What did Susan do to deserve this?

John & Sherry are two children who grew up traumatized in a home punctuated by the daily bouts of violence and beatings their alcoholic father inflicted on their helpless mother.

Jill suffers from cirrhosis of the liver. Cirrhosis is caused by alcohol, and kills 10,000 to 24,000 people a year [1] and is entirely preventable.

Jack – a two year old – is the latest victim of a drunk driver. What did Jack do to deserve this?

While these people are fictitious, the startling gash that alcohol cuts across America every day is all too real. The actual statistics are shocking and at the same time sobering.

Deaths

"Alcohol and other drugs are a factor in 45.1 percent of all fatal automobile crashes" [2]

"Between 47 percent and 65 percent of adult drowning and 59 percent of fatal falls are associated with alcohol." [3]

"An estimated 75 percent of esophageal cancers in the United States are attributable to chronic, excessive alcohol consumption" [4}

"Nearly 50 percent of cancers of the mouth, pharynx, and larynx are associated with heavy drinking." [4]

"25 to 40 percent of all Americans in general hospital beds (that is not in a maternity or intensive care unit bed) are being treated for complications of alcoholism." [5]

"Twenty-eight percent of all admissions to one large metropolitan hospital's intensive care units (ICUs) were related to ATOD problems (9 percent alcohol, 14 percent tobacco, and 5 percent other drugs). The ATOD-related admissions were much more severe than the other 72 percent of admissions, requiring 4.2 days in ICU versus 2.8 days as well as being much more expensive—about 63 percent greater than the average cost for other ICU admissions." [5] [6]

Intoxicants also play a big role in dysfunctional families, the breakup of families, casual sex & abortions, domestic violence, child abuse and incest. Here are some more unfortunate statistics.

"In 1987, 64 percent of all reported child abuse and neglect cases in New York City were associated with parental AOD [alcohol and other drugs] abuse." [7]

"A study of 472 women by the Research Institute on Addictions in Buffalo, NY, found that 87 percent of alcoholic women had been physically or sexually abused as children, compared to 59 percent of the nonalcoholic women surveyed (Miller and Downs, 1993)." [8]

"A 1993 study of more than 2,000 American couples found rates of domestic violence were almost 15 times higher in households where husbands were described as often drunk as opposed to never drunk." [9]

"Battered women are at increased risk of attempting suicide, abusing alcohol and other drugs, depression, and abusing their own children." [10]

"Alcohol is present in more than 50 percent of all incidents of domestic violence." [10]

"A survey of high school students found that 18 percent of females and 39 percent of males say it is acceptable for a boy to force sex if the girl is stoned or drunk." [11]

Intoxicants also affect mental health & suicide statistics in a big way.

"In one study of youthful suicide, drug and alcohol abuse was the most common characteristic of those who attempted suicide; fully 70 percent of these young people frequently used alcohol and/or other drugs." [12]

"Approximately 10 percent of adult dementia in the United States is a result of alcohol-related brain damage." [13]

How about crime? Intoxicants play a deadly role here too.

"Alcohol is a key factor in up to 68 percent of manslaughters, 62 percent of assaults, 54 percent of murders/attempted murders, 48 percent of robberies, and 44 percent of burglaries." [14]

"Among jail inmates, 42.2 percent of those convicted of rape reported being under the influence of alcohol or alcohol and other drugs at the time of the offense." [15]

"Over 60 percent of men and 50 percent of women arrested for property crimes (burglary, larceny, robbery) in 1990, who were voluntarily tested, tested positive for illicit drug use." [16]

"In 1987, 64 percent of all reported child abuse and neglect cases in New York City were associated with parental AOD [alcohol and other drugs] abuse." [17]

"A study prepared by The Lewin Group for the National Institute on Drug Abuse and the National Institute on Alcohol Abuse and Alcoholism estimated the total economic cost of alcohol and drug abuse to be $245.7 billion for 1992. Of this cost, $97.7 billion was due to drug abuse. This estimate includes substance abuse treatment and prevention costs as well as other health care costs, costs associated with reduced job productivity or lost earnings, and other costs to society, such as crime and social welfare" [18]

These costs have only gone up every year. And of course, these numbers do not even begin to suggest the magnitude of the personal and emotional cost and turmoil of intoxicants in America.

It can be a sad tale for many who find themselves in the darkness of intoxicant abuse. Looking back, it must be a huge shock and surprise to them - the fact that first innocuous drink or smoked joint could have begun that path of ever spiraling decent into the terrible predicament that some may now be trying so desperately to escape. After all, no one ever imagined it could happen to them! Certainly, innocent third parties, like their families, may be shaking their heads, never having imagined such a path would be craved out in life for them. [19]

Muslims note, that Islam has dramatically reduced alcohol consumption in several societies, nations, and communities and has paved over some of the potentially dark trap doors that could be stumbled upon leading to intoxicant abuse. Muslim societies, more so than other communities, have been able to successfully limit intoxicants in their societies since Islam prohibited it over 1400 years ago (Quran 5:90 & 2:219). Muslims would point out that today, even though not every Muslim follows Islamic injunctions prohibiting alcohol, an astoundingly large number do. Because most Muslims do not drink, it is very likely that well over a billion teetotalers have been created as a direct result of Islam.

Sources:
National Institute on Alcohol Abuse and Alcoholism
— NIAAA see
www.niaaa.nih.gov/publications/alalerts.htm

National Clearinghouse for Alcohol and Drug
Information/Center for Substance Abuse Prevention
NCADI — CSAP see
http://www.samhsa.gov/centers/csap/csap.html

National Institute on Drug Abuse — NIDA see www.
nida.nih.gov/.

References:
[1] NIAAA – Alcohol Alert no. 42,

[2] NCADI/CSAP – Making the Link, Impaired Driving,
Injury, and Trauma and Alcohol and other Drugs.
Spring 1995, NCADI Inventory Number ML004.

[3] NCADI/CSAP – Making the Link, Impaired Driving,
Injury, and Trauma and Alcohol and other Drugs.
Spring 1995, NCADI Inventory Number ML004.

[4] NIAAA—Alcohol Alert no. 21

[5] NCADI/CSAP: Making the Link: Health care costs,
the deficit, and alcohol, tobacco, and other drugs.
Spring 1995, NCADI Inventory Number ML007

[6] NCADI/CSAP: Making the Link: Health care costs,
the deficit, and alcohol, tobacco, and other drugs.
Spring 1995, NCADI Inventory Number ML007

[7] NCADI/CSAP: Making the Link; Domestic violence

and alcohol and other drugs. Spring 1995, NCADI Inventory Number ML001

[8] NCADI/CSAP: Making the Link; Domestic violence and alcohol and other drugs. Spring 1995, NCADI Inventory Number ML001.

[9] NCADI/CSAP: Making the Link; Domestic violence and alcohol and other drugs. Spring 1995, NCADI Inventory Number ML001

[10] NCADI/CSAP: Making the Link; Domestic violence and alcohol and other drugs. Spring 1995, NCADI Inventory Number ML001

[11] NCADI/CSAP: Making the Link: Sex under the influence of alcohol and other drugs. Spring 1995, NCADI Inventory Number ML005

[12] NCADI/CSAP: Making the Link: Alcohol and other drugs suicide. Spring 1995, NCADI Inventory Number ML009

[13] NCADI/CSAP: Making the Link: Alcohol, tobacco, and other drugs and mental health, Spring 1995, NCADI Inventory Number ML012

[14] NCADI/CSAP: Making the Link: Violence and crime and alcohol and other drugs. Spring 1995, NCADI Inventory Number ML002

[15] NCADI/CSAP: Making the Link: Violence and crime and alcohol and other drugs. Spring 1995, NCADI Inventory Number ML002

[16] NCADI/CSAP: Making the Link: Violence and crime and alcohol and other drugs. Spring 1995, NCADI Inventory Number ML002

[17] NCADI/CSAP: Making the Link: Violence and crime and alcohol and other drugs. Spring 1995, NCADI Inventory Number ML002

[18] National Institute on Drug Abuse, National Institutes of Health, "Costs to Society" [1356

[19] As an side note: Unrelated (e.g. third party) effects draw some parallels with an area of economics that deals with "externalities." Where prices are "disconnected" from capturing important cost or revenue information associated with or tagged to "non-transacting" parties.

Section V: Islamic Resources

"Show gentleness, for if gentleness is found in anything, it beautifies it and when it is taken out from anything it damages it."
(Sunan Abu Dawud Book 41, Number 4790)

"Riches does not mean, having a great amount of property, but riches is self-contentment." (Sahih Bukhari 8.453)

"Do not be people without minds of your own, saying that if others treat you well you will treat them well and that if they do wrong you will do wrong; but accustom yourselves to do good if people do good and not to do wrong if they do evil." (Tirmidhi 5129)

"There is a piece of flesh in the body if it becomes good (reformed) the whole body becomes good but if it gets spoilt the whole body gets spoilt and that is the heart." (Bukhari Vo 1, Bk 2, #49)

"Take advantage of five things before five others: your youth before your old age, your health before your sickness, your wealth before your poverty, your free time before you become occupied, and your life before your death." (Tirmidhi)

Islam on the Internet & Other Resources

By F. Kamal

Warning: Much of the information one encounters on Islam (particularly on the internet) may be biased, distorted, exaggerated, inaccurate, or incomplete. The primary sources of Islam are the Quran (Muslim holy book) and the Sunnah (example) of Prophet Muhammad. These primary sources have been, and are interpreted, by Muslim scholars (the ulema.) When one is first learning about Islam, one should try to find the most knowledgeable, practicing Muslim one can to answer one's questions, as well as to locate an accessible mosque (Muslim house of worship).

THE QURAN

The Quran is the holy book of the Muslims. "Quran" is an Arabic word that means "that which is to be read" which shows the importance of active, continuous learning in Islam. According to Muslim belief, the first revealed word of the Quran was "Iqra" meaning "read" or "recite" in Arabic. Muslims believe that the Quran was revealed by God to Muhammad through Archangel Gabriel and that the Quran is the exact, unaltered word of God and has not been changed in the last 1400 years. It is preserved in the original. It is in Arabic. Three reputable English translations are by 1) M. Pickthall, 2) A. Yusuf Ali, and 3) Muhammad Asad. English translations are usually the preferred starting points for non-Arabic English speaking readers.

But stay clear of questionable translations (ask a knowledgeable Muslim if you are unsure). Be aware that even the best translations cannot be a substitute for the original Arabic and may contain errors. Therefore if you read a translation and do not understand something, try and ask an Islamic scholar or knowledgeable Muslim about it. For Quran on the internet click on http://www.usc.edu/dept/MSA/quran/.

PROPHET MUHAMMAD

"Muhammad: His Life Based on the Earliest Sources" by Martin Lings is a general book about the Prophet.

"The Message" is a video about the life of the Prophet and is an excellent starting point for many people. There is also a documentary, entitled ""Muhammad: Legacy of a prophet" by PBS.

BASICS ABOUT ISLAM (QUICK INFORMATION)

Discover Islam Poster Exhibit . Good 1st Internet tour for non-Muslims.
(http://www.discoverislam.com/)

FOR THOSE NEW TO OR INTERESTED IN ISLAM

1. Islamicity. General Introductory topics & issues. (www.islam.org).

2. www.jannah.org. Another Islamic website. Section on Muslim women.

3. Some Ahmed Deedat videos may appeal to some, may not to others. (e.g. Mixed reviews.)

SOME INTRODUCTORY BOOKS ON ISLAM

1. "What Every Christian Should know about Islam" by Ruqaiyyah Maqsood. Includes responses to frequently asked questions by non-Muslims.

2. "The Complete Idiot's Guide to Understanding Islam" by Yahiya Emerick.

3. "What Everyone Should Know about Islam and Muslims " by Suzanne Haneef. General.

4. "The Koran for Dummies" by Sohaib Sultan.

Some non-Muslims may prefer to read works on Islam by non-Muslims. Here are some possibilities.

1. By a Christian author: "More in common than you think. The Bridge between Islam and Christianity" by Bill Baker. Includes answers to questions frequently asked by non-Muslims. ISBN: 0910643016.

2. By a Jewish author: "Jesus and Muhammad: The

Chapter 21

Parallel Sayings." By Joey Green. ISBN: 1-56975-326-1.

Chapter Updates (if any):

Easily-Understand-Islam.com

Note: Unfortunately, accurate Islamic books/material is sometimes difficult to find in one's local bookstores or library. We will try to maintain links for buying Islamic books and videos at

www.Easily-Understand-Islam.com

You can also try a national Muslim organization like ISNA (www.isna.net), your local mosque or a (practicing) Muslim friend to get these resources.

Disclaimer: Links and references to books and websites in this book are presented solely as a convenience to the reader. Such presentations definitely do NOT constitute endorsement or complete agreement with the entire content or opinions of such books, organizations, individuals, multimedia items and websites. It should also be noted that websites change over time becoming less, or more, useful in time.

Website & Feedback

This book has a website
http://www.EasilyUnderstandIslam.com
http://www.Easily-Understand-Islam.com

Upon visiting, one should see text indicating that it is the official website for this book. Do visit the website and give us some feedback.

You can also subscribe to our mailing list and join our RSS feed at the website.

Epilogue

One book can go only so far. We recognize that various individuals including writers, webmasters, teachers, etc. may be reading this book. In the spirit of cross pollinating ideas, the open source revolution in software, and in order to promote this book and further the understanding of Islam, we have decided to experiment by not enforcing our copyright of our original work in the following chapters: Chapter 1 & 2 in English (only) *if* you follow certain rules. Depending on our experience we may choose to add to this mix.

Rules: The original message remains intact (not distorted -- solely as determined by us) and that a proper citation including the chapter number, title, ISBN, and a clickable hyperlink to the website of this book be prominently given and separately inserted for each of the two chapters used. This option is currently *only available in English for chapters 1 & 2* (check the website for the exact details, including any future updates on this).

Reflections

Upon first lifting a pen, a Muslim author is very much aware of his inadequacy in presenting the subject matter, and his pen is stilled. While the weight must be discharged with hard work and research, a Muslim author realizes that ultimately God is the Source of all Goodness. Therefore the author would not have the courage to continue writing without resorting to prayer to ask for God's help with the task. One hopes this prayer is at least partly, if not fully, answered. If there is any good in the work it is by God's immense Grace since ultimately God is the Source of all Goodness. Where there are mistakes, they reflect a human's very real limitations and ignorance – and opportunity for growth. We ask that our readers understand our limitations, and we ask God to forgive us our many weaknesses.

F. Kamal

Index

U

V

W

Z

Breinigsville, PA USA
04 March 2010
233642BV00001B/38/P